THE MOST REQUESTED
Movie Songs

Cherry Lane Music Company
Director of Publications/Project Editor: Mark Phillips

ISBN 978-1-60378-974-5

Visit our website at www.cherrylaneprint.com

CONTENTS

An Affair to Remember
(Our Love Affair)
from AN AFFAIR TO REMEMBER

Words by
Harold Adamson and Leo McCarey

Music by Harry Warren

love was born with our first em - brace, And a
messe ar - dente du pre - mier bai - ser, Qui nous

page was torn out of time and space. Our
lie, tous deux, pour l'é - ter - ni - té D'un

love af - fair, may it al - ways be a
bel a - mour tou - jours gran - dis - sant, Qui

flame to burn through e - ter - ni - ty. So,
dé - fie - ra les é - preuves du temps. Trou -

take my hand, with a fer - vent pray'r, That
vons la joie, res - te dans mes bras, Que

we may live and we may share a
nous vi - vions un bel a - mour, Af -

love af - fair to re - mem - ber. Our
faire de cœur, qu'on n'ou - blie pas. Ce

ber.
pas.

6

Alfie
Theme from the Paramount Picture ALFIE

Words by Hal David

Music by Burt Bacharach

Very slowly, rubato

What's it all a-bout, Al - fie? _____ Is it just for the mo - ment we live? What's it all a-bout _____ when you sort it out, _____ Al - fie? _____

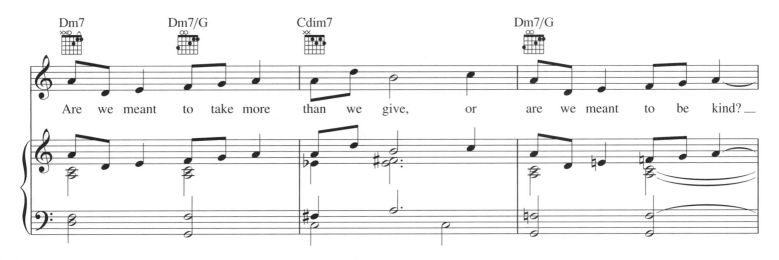

Are we meant to take more than we give, or are we meant to be kind? ___

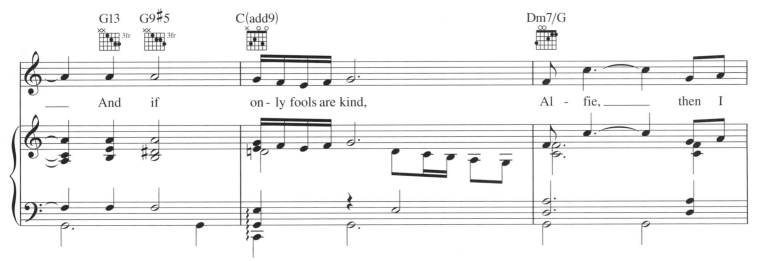

___ And if on - ly fools are kind, Al - fie, _____ then I

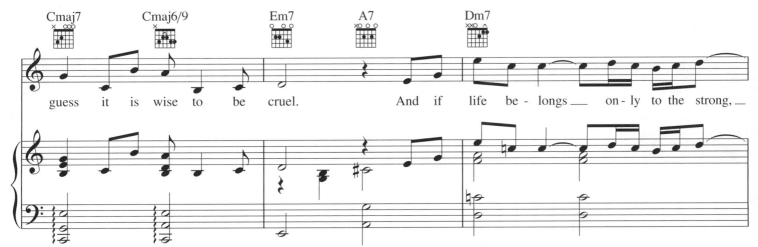

guess it is wise to be cruel. And if life be - longs ___ on - ly to the strong, ___

___ Al - fie, ___ what will you lend on an old gold - en rule? As

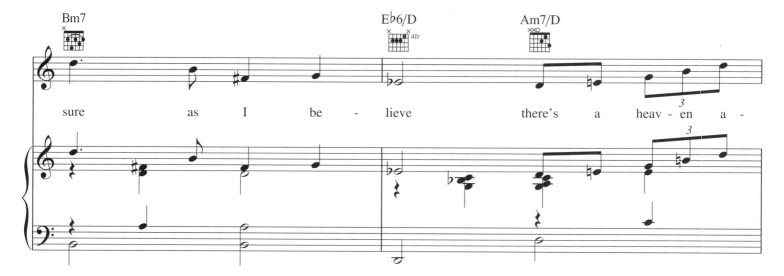

sure as I be-lieve there's a heav-en a-

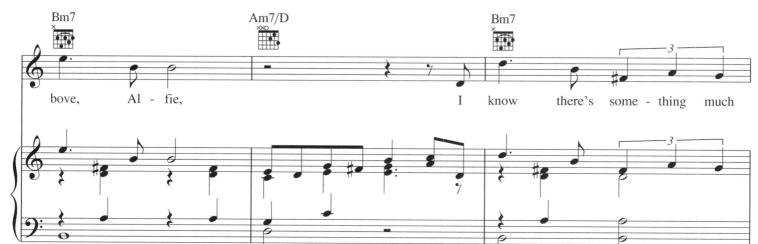

bove, Al-fie, I know there's some-thing much

more, some-thing e-ven non-be-liev-ers can be-lieve in.

I be-lieve in love, Al-fie.____ With-out true love we just ex-

And I Am Telling You I'm Not Going

from DREAMGIRLS

Lyric by Tom Eyen

Music by Henry Krieger

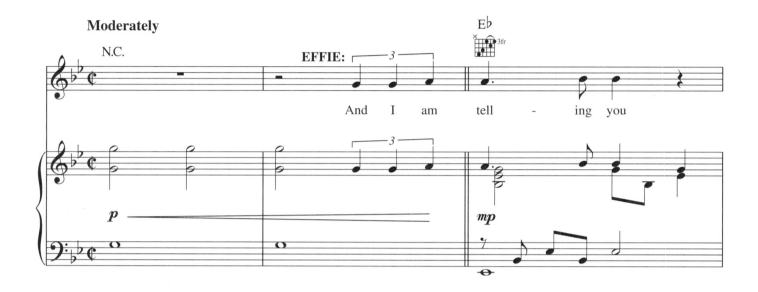

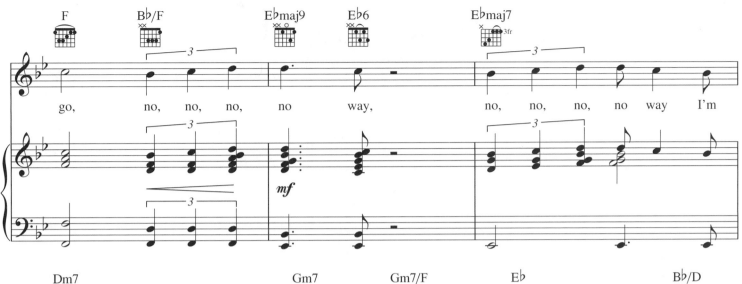

go, no, no, no, no way, no, no, no, no way I'm

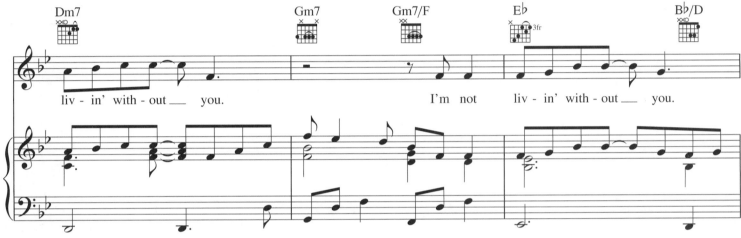

liv - in' with - out ___ you. I'm not liv - in' with - out ___ you.

I don't want to be ___ free. ___ I'm

stay - in', ___ I'm stay - in', and you, and you,

you're gon - na love _____ me. _____ Ooh, _____

you're gon - na love _____ me.

And _____ I am

tell - ing you   I'm not go - ing, _____

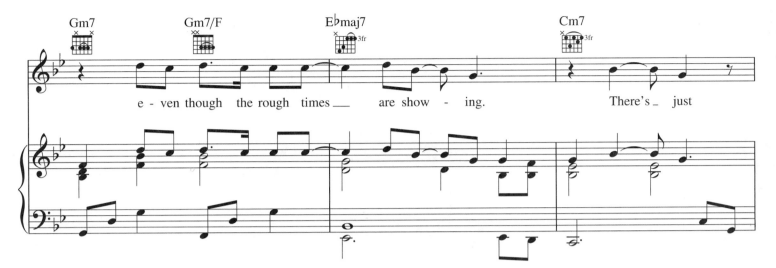

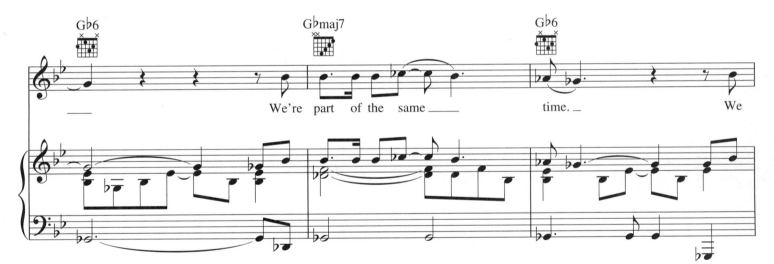

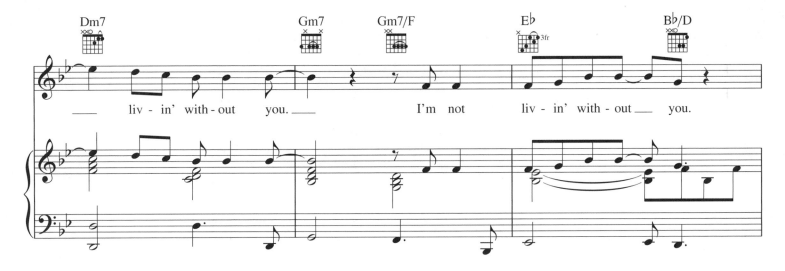

liv - in' with - out you. ___ I'm not liv - in' with - out ___ you.

You see, there's just no way, there's no ___ way. ___

Funky

Tear down the moun - tains, yell, ___ scream and shout. You can

say what you want, ___ I'm not walk - in' out. Stop all the riv - ers, push, ___

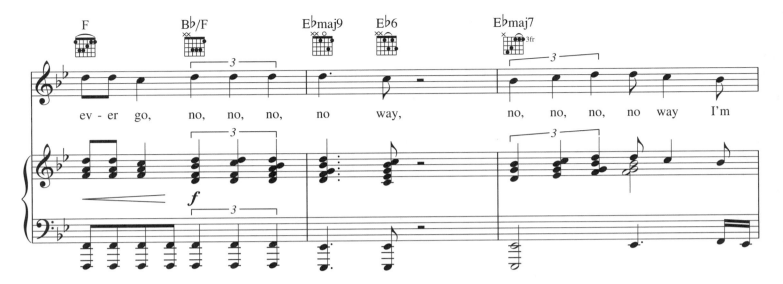

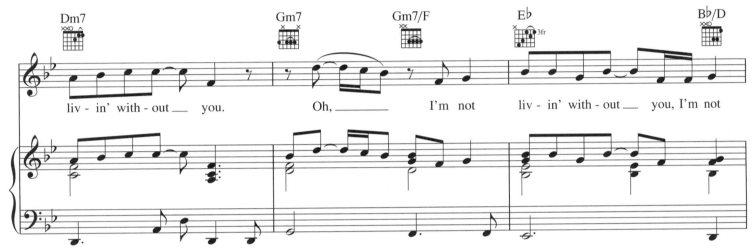

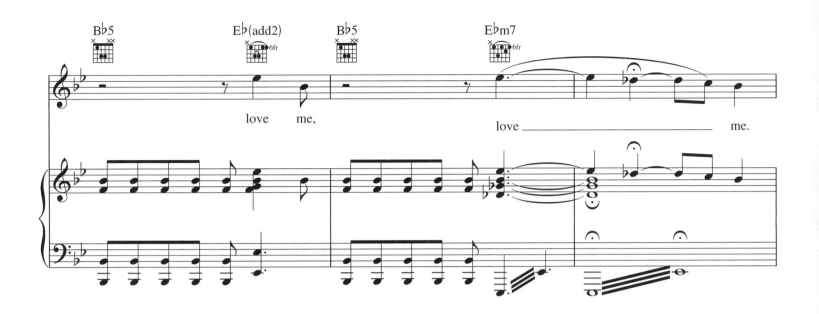

love me, love   me.

Freely

You're gon - na love

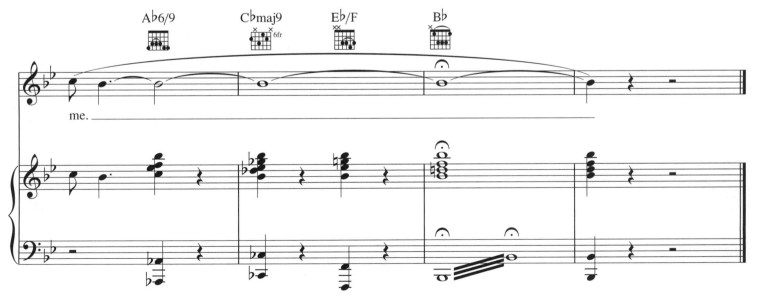

me.

Arthur's Theme
(Best That You Can Do)
from ARTHUR an ORION PICTURES release through WARNER BROS.

Words and Music by
Burt Bacharach, Carole Bayer Sager,
Christopher Cross and Peter Allen

Moderately

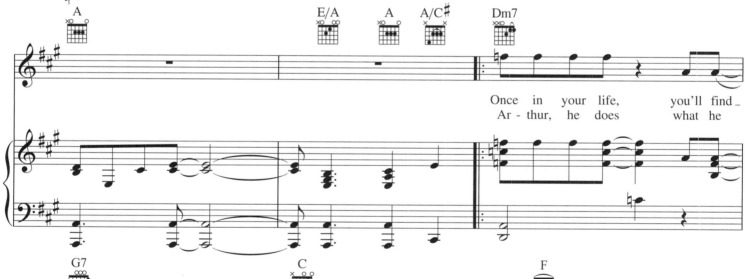

Once in your life, you'll find __
Ar - thur, he does find what he

_____ her, some - one who turns __ your heart a - round, and
pleas - es. All of his life, __ his mas - ter's toys, and

next thing you know, you're clos - in' down the town.
deep in his heart, he's just, he's just a boy.

Wake up and she's _____ still with _____
Liv - in' his life _____ one day _____

_____ you,
_____ at a time, he's

e - ven though you left her way _____
show - ing him - self a real -

_____ a - cross town. You're won - der - in' to your -
- ly good time. He's laugh - in' a - bout the

self, hey, what-'ve I found?
way they want him to be.

When you get caught be-tween the moon and New York

Cit - y, I know it's cra - zy,

but it's true. ___

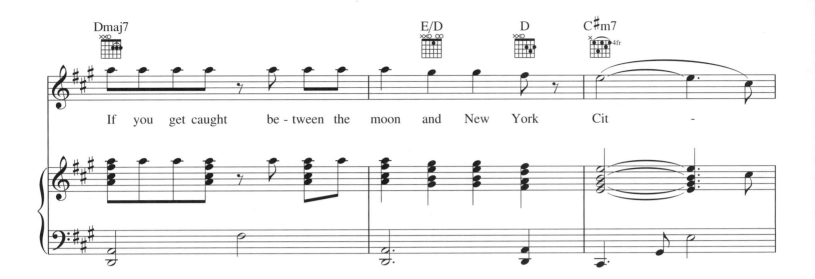

If you get caught be - tween the moon and New York Cit -

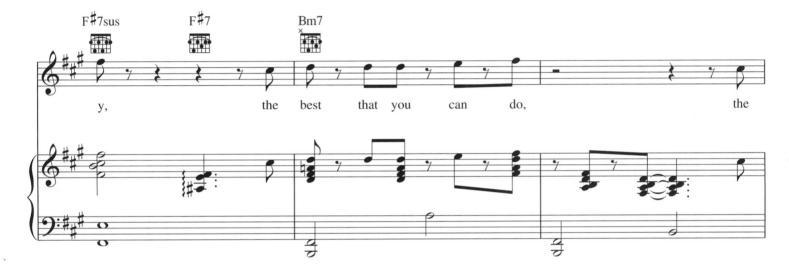

y, the best that you can do, the

best that you can do is fall ___ in love. ___

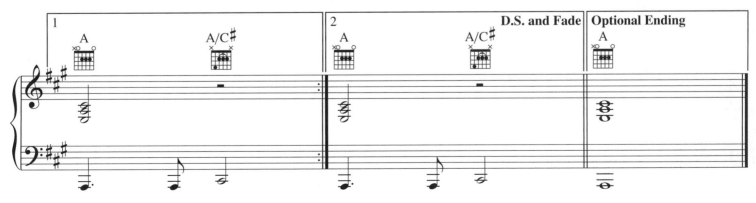

As Time Goes By

from CASABLANCA

Words and Music by
Herman Hupfeld

Liltingly

26

Because You Loved Me

from UP CLOSE AND PERSONAL

Words and Music by
Diane Warren

Slowly ♩ = 76   *Verse:*

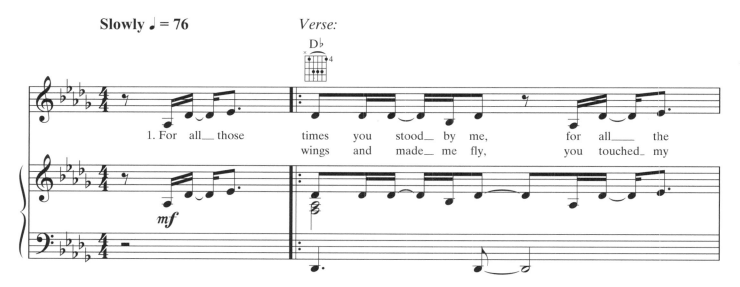

1. For all__ those times you stood__ by me, for all__ the
wings and made__ me fly, you touched__ my

truth that you made me see, for all__ the joy you brought to my life,__ for all__ the
hand, I could touch the sky. I lost__ my faith you gave it back to me. You said__ no

wrong that you__ made right, for ev-ery__ dream you made__ come true, for all__ the
star was out__ of reach, you stood__ by__ me and I__ stood tall. I had__ your

love I found_ in you,____ I'll be for-ev-er thank-ful, ba-by.
love, I had_ it all.____ I'm grate-ful for_ each day____ you gave me.

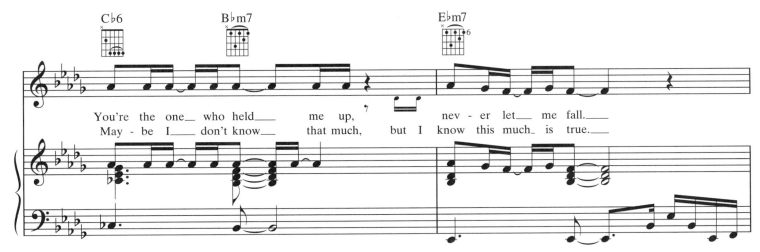

You're the one_ who held____ me up, nev-er let__ me fall.____
May-be I__ don't know____ that much, but I know this much_ is true.____

You're the one_ who saw____ me through, through it all.____
I was blessed_ be-cause____ I was loved by you.____
You were_ my

% *Chorus:*

strength when I____ was weak, you were_ my voice when I could-n't speak. You were_ my

eyes when I could-n't see, you saw__ the best there was__ in me, lift-ed__ me__

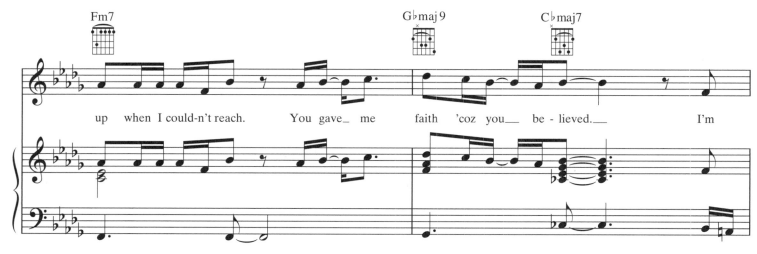

up when I could-n't reach. You gave__ me faith 'coz you__ be-lieved.__ I'm

To Coda ⊕ 1.

ev-ery-thing__ I am be-cause__ you loved__ me. 2. You gave__ me

2. *Bridge:*

loved__ me. You were al-ways there__ for me, the ten-der wind__ that car-ried__ me. A

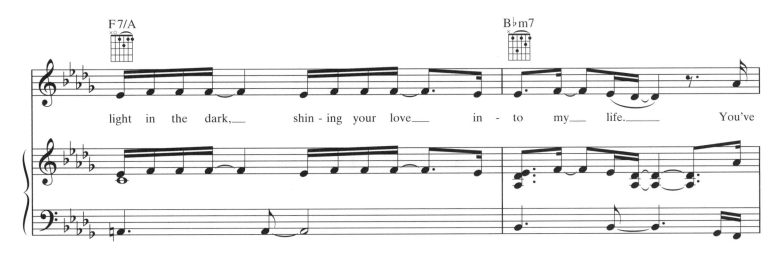

light in the dark,___ shin - ing your love___ in - to my___ life.___ You've

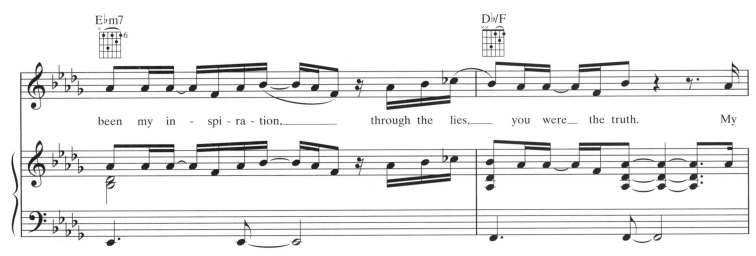

been my in - spi - ra - tion,___ through the lies,___ you were___ the truth. My

D.S. % al Coda

world is a bet - ter place be - cause___ of you.___ You were___ my

Coda

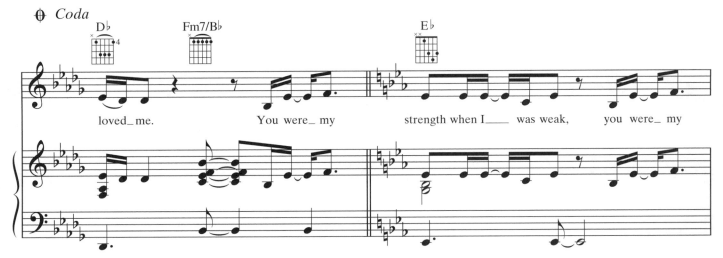

loved___ me. You were___ my strength when I___ was weak, you were___ my

voice when I could-n't speak. You were___ my eyes when I could-n't see, you saw___ the

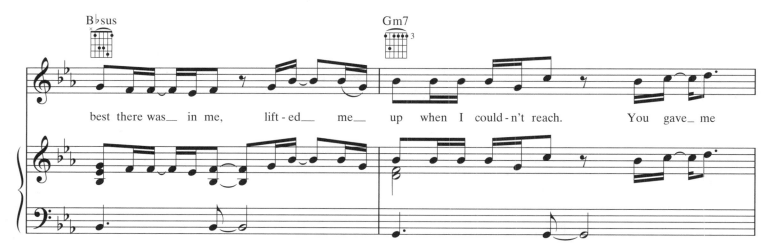

best there was___ in me, lift-ed___ me___ up when I could-n't reach. You gave___ me

faith 'coz you___ be-lieved.___ I'm ev-ery-thing___ I am be-cause___ you

loved___ me. I'm ev-ery-thing___ I am be-cause___ you loved___ me.___

Born Free

from the Columbia Pictures' Release BORN FREE

Words by Don Black

Music by John Barry

Stay free, _____ where no walls di - vide you, _____ you're free as a

roar - ing tide, so there's no need to __ hide. _____

Born free, _____ and life is worth liv - ing, _____ but on - ly worth

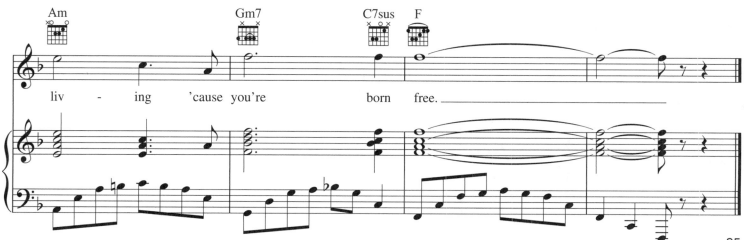

liv - ing 'cause you're born free. _____

Call Me Irresponsible

from the Paramount Picture PAPA'S DELICATE CONDITION

Words by Sammy Cahn

Music by James Van Heusen

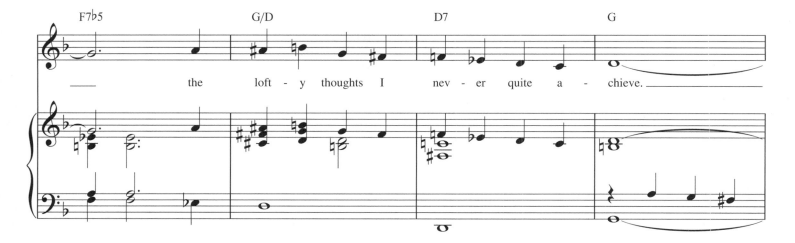

F7♭5   G/D   D7   G

the loft - y thoughts I nev - er quite a - chieve.

Gm   C9   C9♭5   Fmaj9   F6

Each time I'm tak - ing bows 'cause ev - 'ry - thing went well,

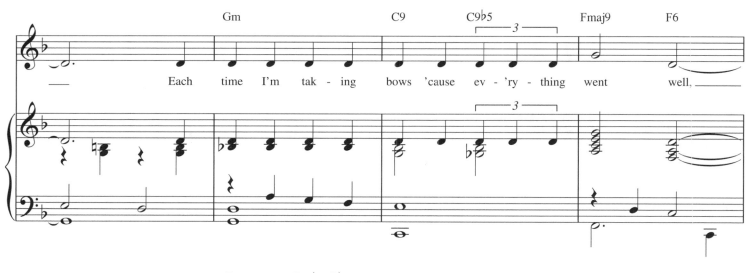

Dm   Dm(maj7)   Dm7/G   G13   C9

things go a - wry, and there am I say - ing I meant well.

decresc.

Slowly, with a steady rhythm

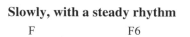

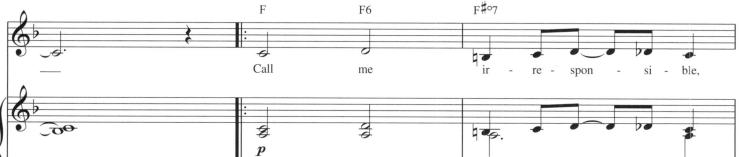

F   F6   F#°7

p

Call me ir - re - spon - si - ble,

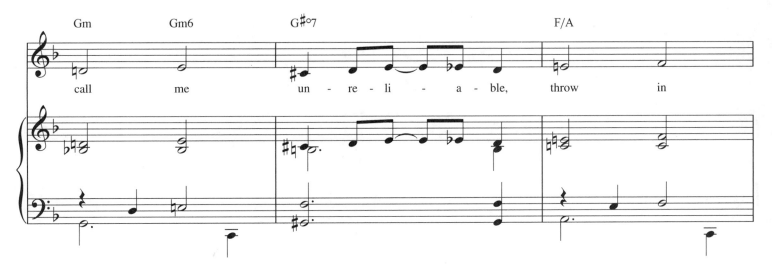

call me un-re-li-a-ble, throw in

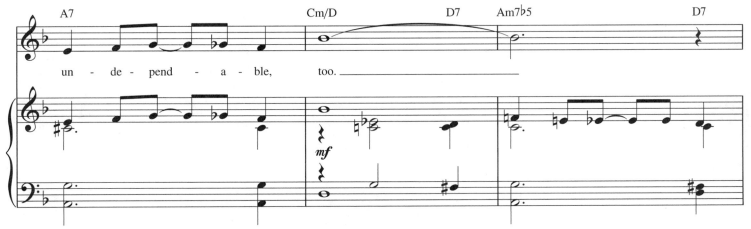

un-de-pend-a-ble, too. _____

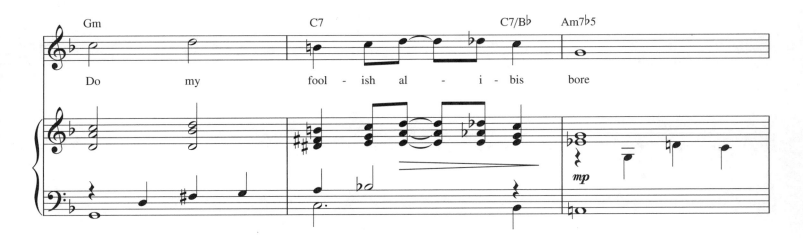

Do my fool-ish al-i-bis bore

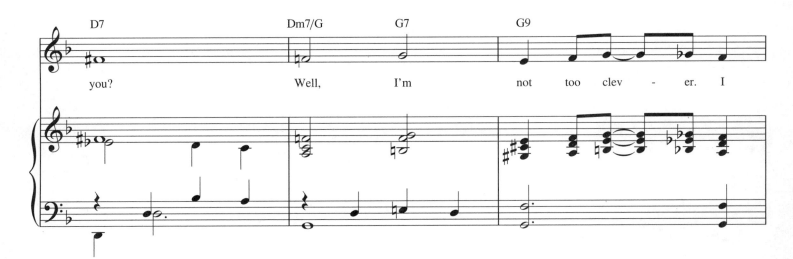

you? Well, I'm not too clev-er. I

yes, I'm un-re-li-a-ble, but it's un-de-ni-a-bly true ____ I'm ir-re-spon-si-bly mad for you! ____ you! ____

A Certain Smile

from A CERTAIN SMILE

Words by Paul Francis Webster

Music by Sammy Fain

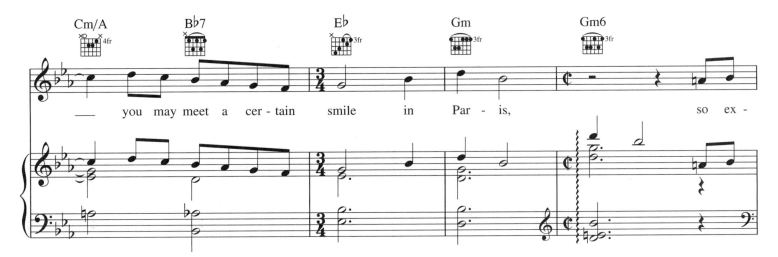

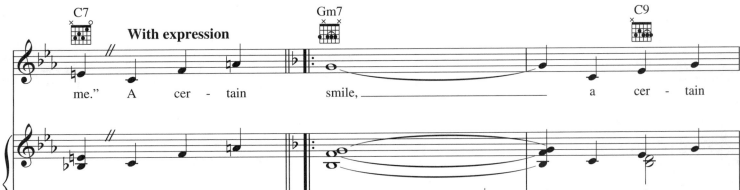

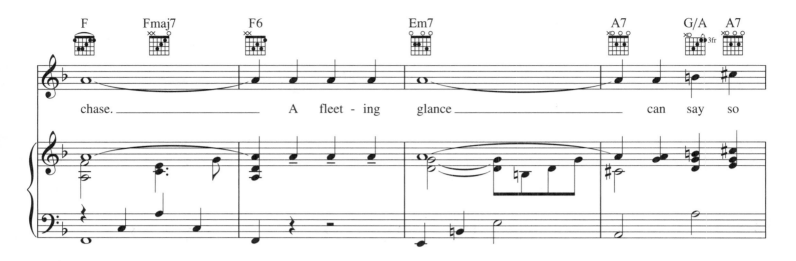

chase. _____ A fleet-ing glance _____ can say so

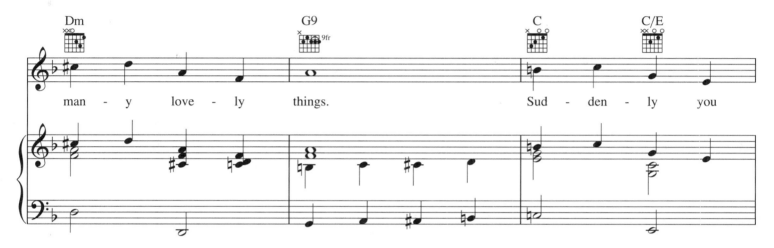

man - y love - ly things. Sud - den - ly you

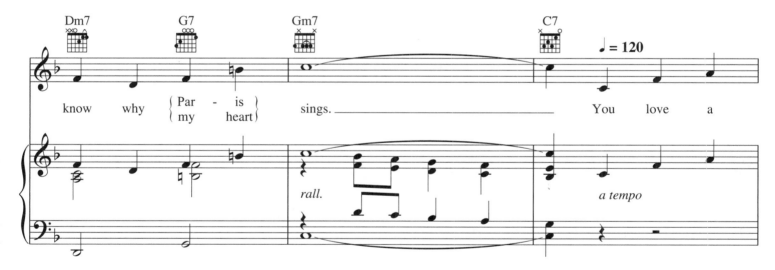

know why { Par - is } sings. _____ You love a
        { my heart }

rall.   a tempo

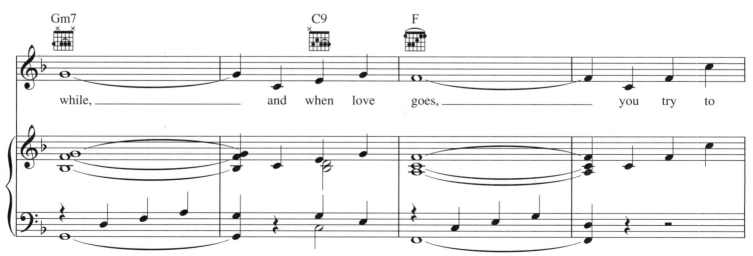

while, _____ and when love goes, _____ you try to

43

Charade

Theme from the Film CHARADE

Words by Johnny Mercer

Music by Henry Mancini

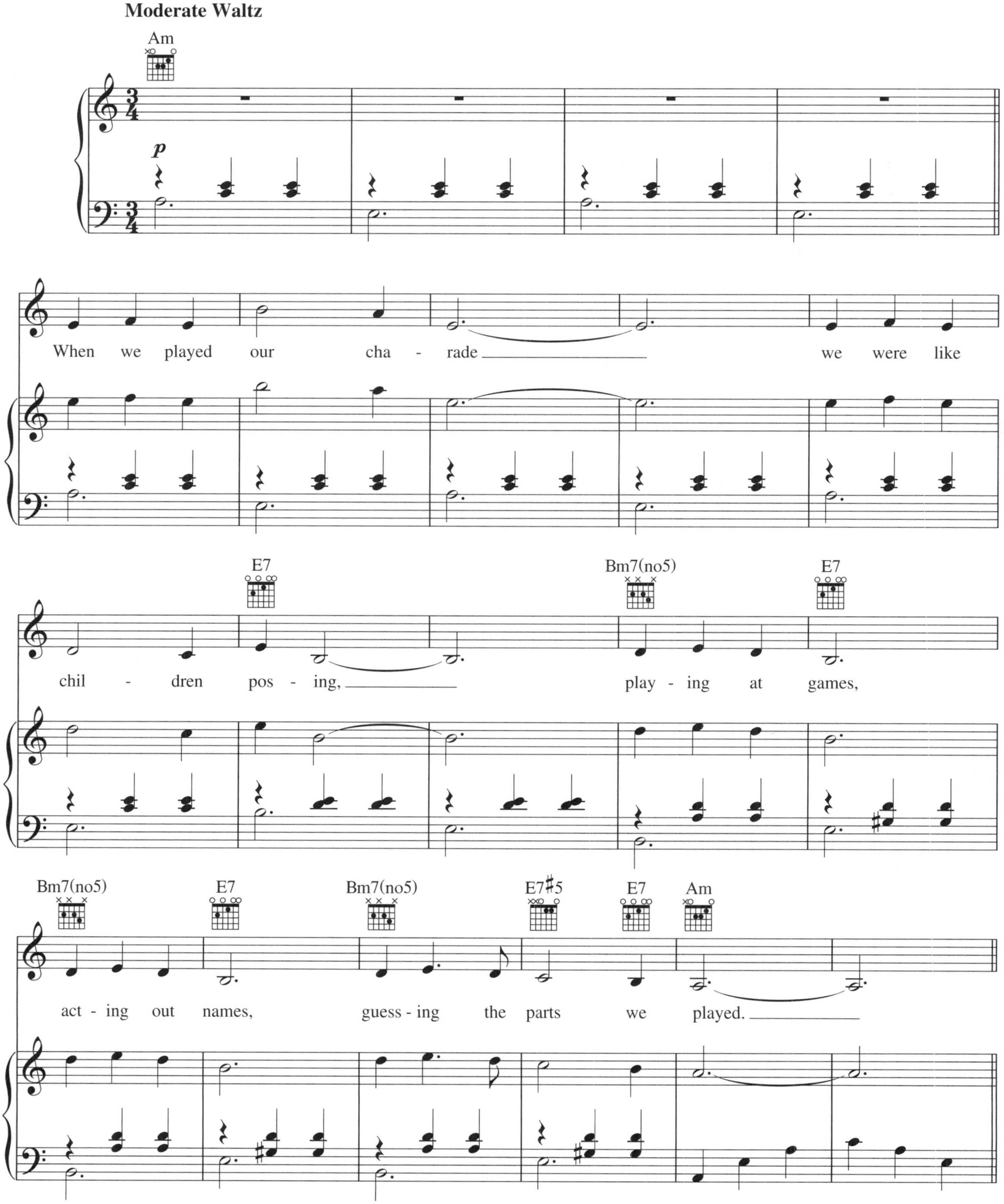

Moderate Waltz
Am
p
When we played our cha - rade
we were like
E7
Bm7(no5)
E7
chil - dren pos - ing,
play - ing at games,
Bm7(no5)
E7
Bm7(no5)
E7♯5
E7
Am
act - ing out names,
guess - ing the parts we played.

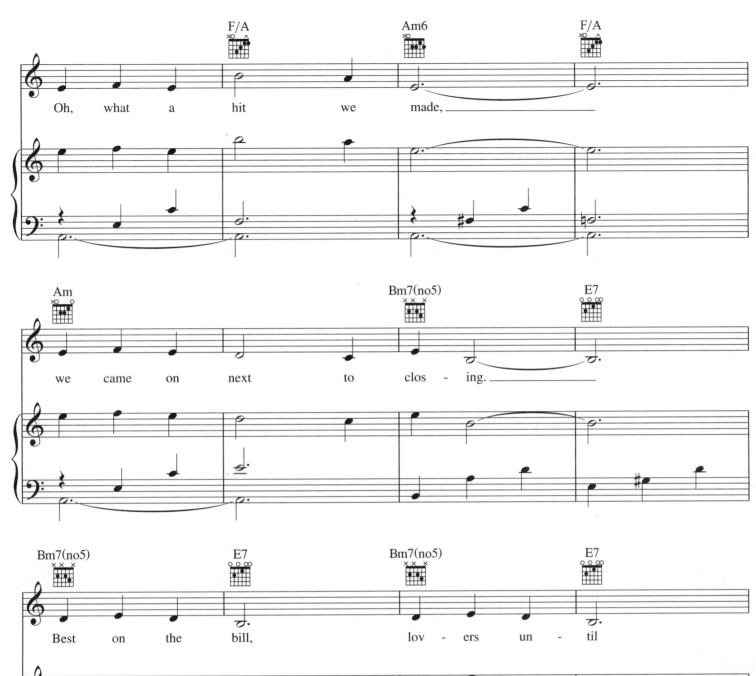

Oh, what a hit we made, _____ we came on next to clos-ing. _____

Best on the bill, lov-ers un-til

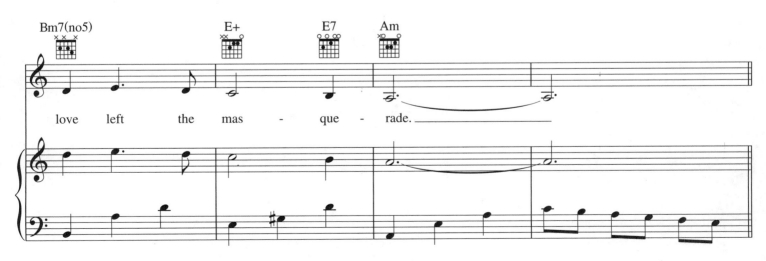

love left the mas-que-rade. _____

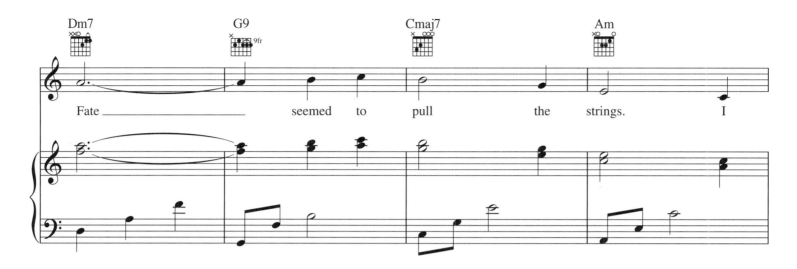

Fate _____ seemed to pull the strings. I

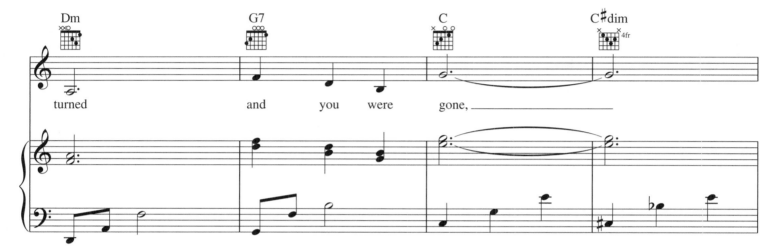

turned and you were gone, _____

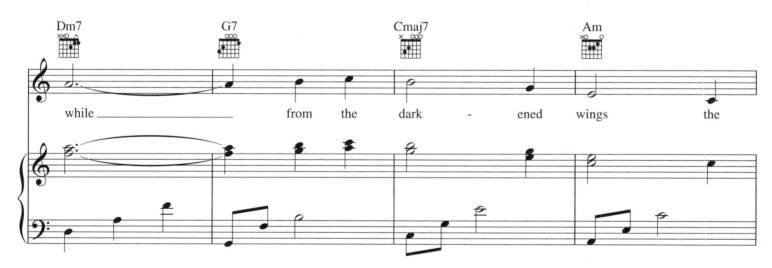

while _____ from the dark - ened wings the

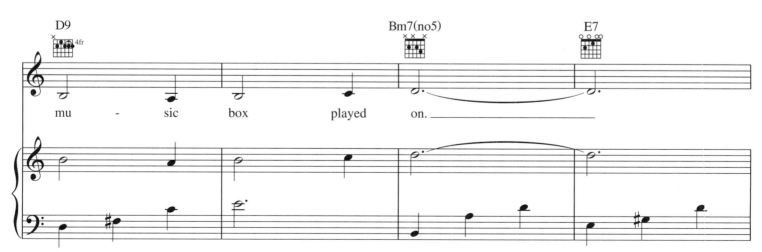

mu - sic box played on. _____

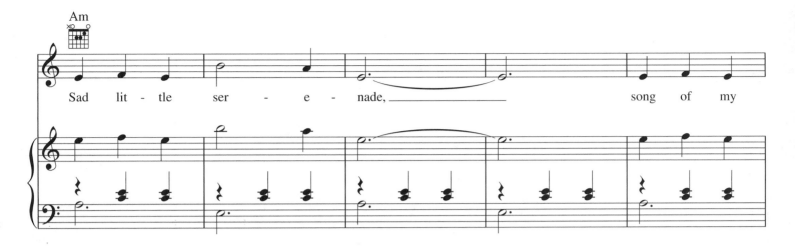

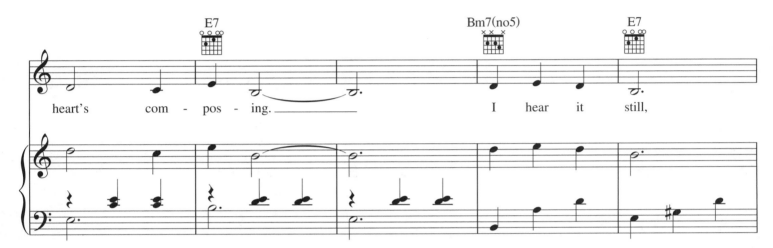

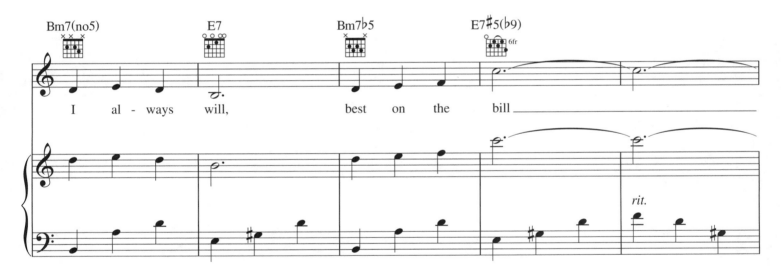

Chariots of Fire

from CHARIOTS OF FIRE

By Vangelis

Moderately

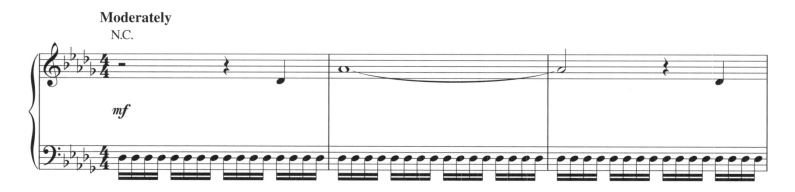

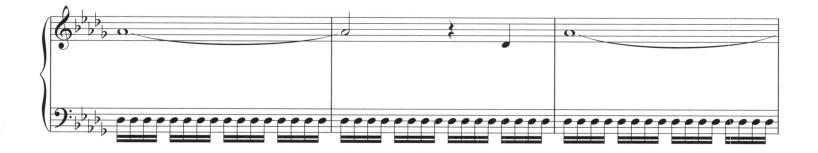

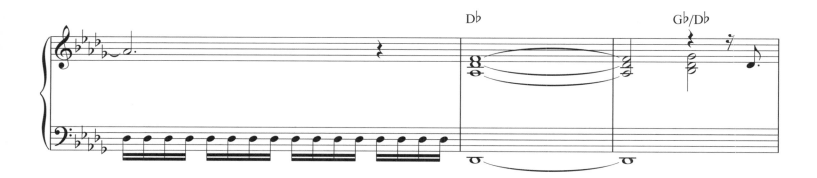

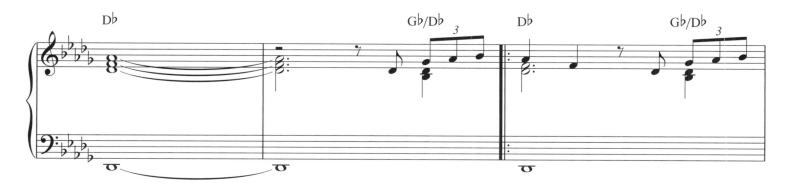

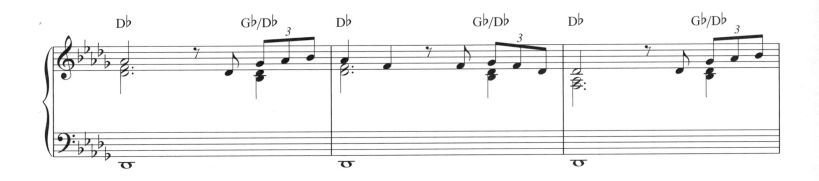

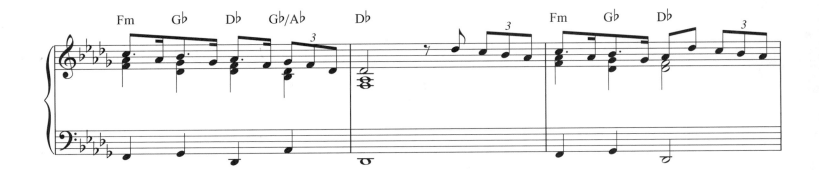

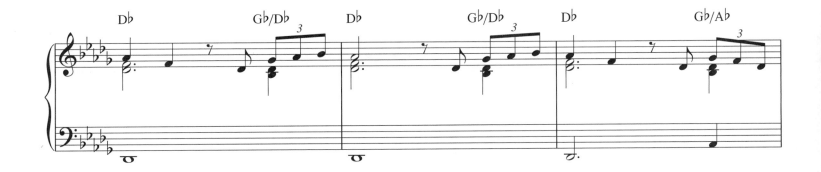

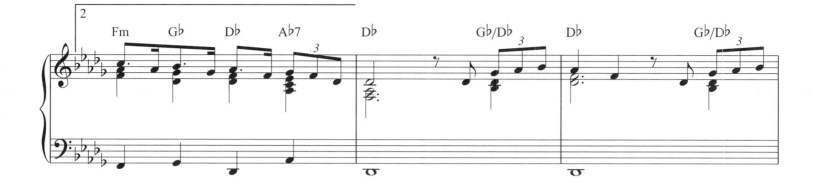

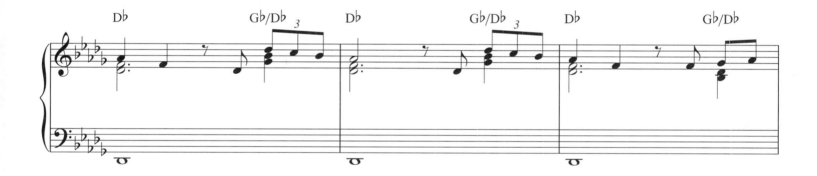

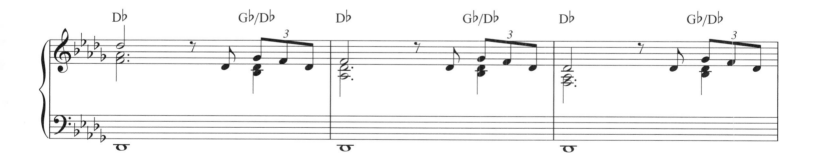

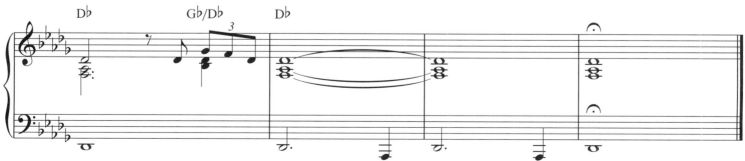

Days of Wine and Roses

Theme from the Film DAYS OF WINE AND ROSES

Lyrics by Johnny Mercer

Music by Henry Mancini

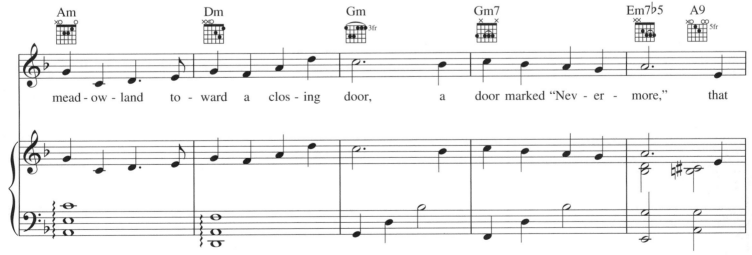

was-n't there be - fore. _____ The lone - ly night dis-

clos - es _____ just a pass-ing breeze _____ filled with mem - o - ries _____

_____ of the gold-en smile that in - tro-duced me to _____ the days of wine and

ros - es and you. _____ The you. _____

Do You Know Where You're Going To?

Theme from MAHOGANY

Words by Gerry Goffin

Music by Michael Masser

Moderately, with expression

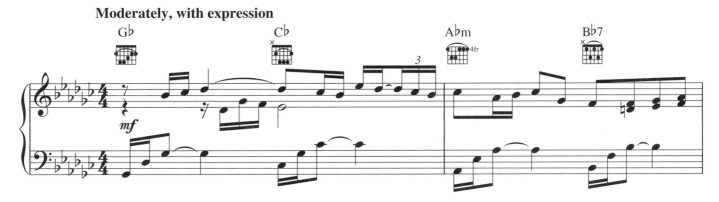

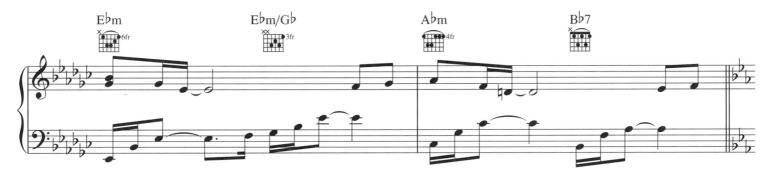

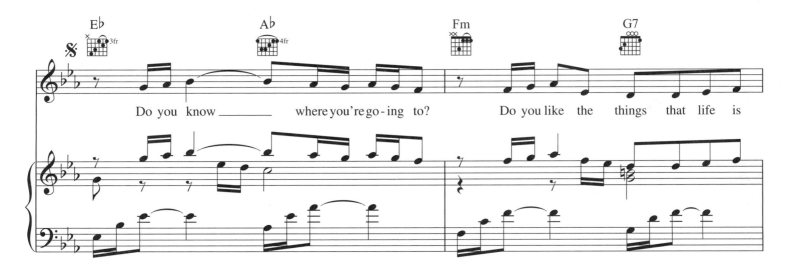

Do you know _____ where you're go-ing to? Do you like the things that life is

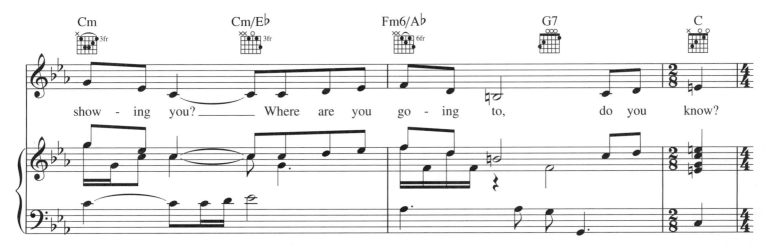

show - ing you? _____ Where are you go - ing to, do you know?

Do you get _____ what you're hop-ing for? When you look be - hind you there's no

To Coda ⊕

o - pen door. _____ What are you hop-ing for, do you

know? Once we were stand - ing still in time,

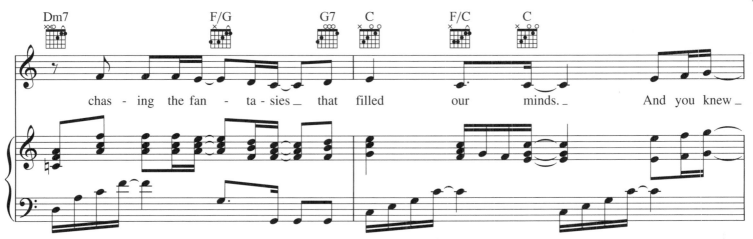

chas - ing the fan - ta - sies ___ that filled our minds. ___ And you knew ___

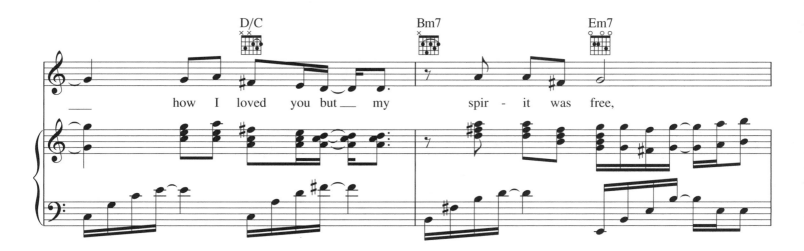

how I loved you but __ my spir - it was free,

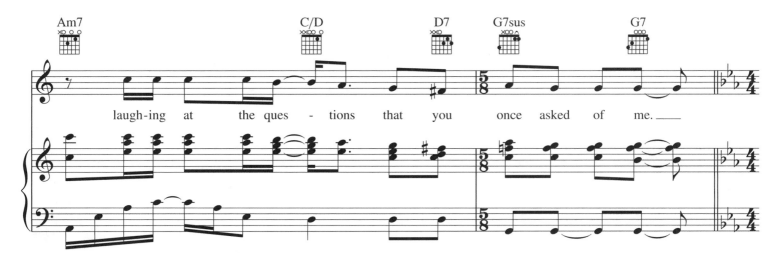

laugh-ing at the ques - tions that you once asked of me. __

Do you know _____ where you're go - ing to? Do you like the things that life is

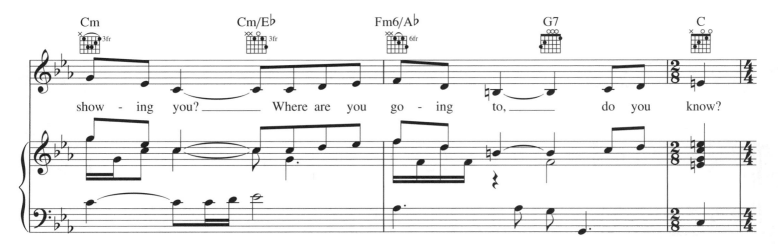

show - ing you? _____ Where are you go - ing to, _____ do you know?

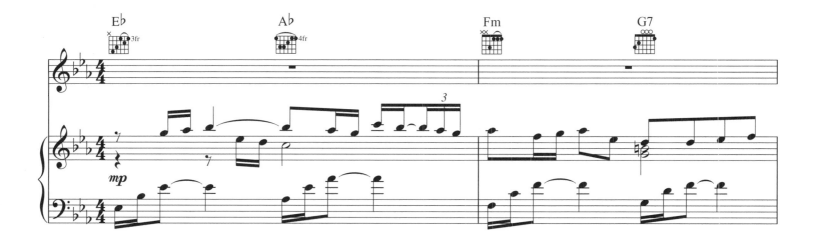

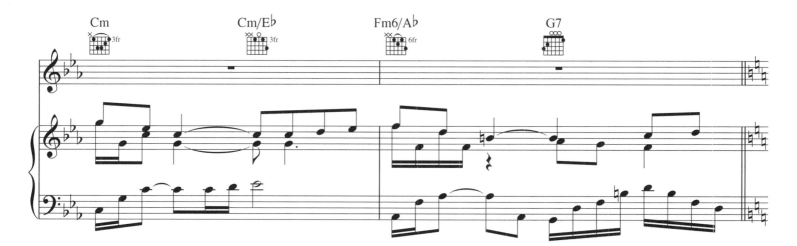

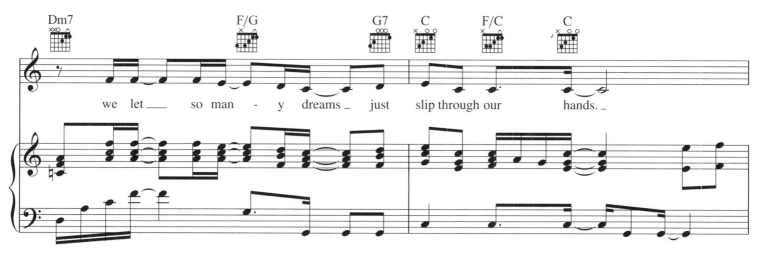

Now _____ look-ing back at all _____ we planned,

we let _____ so man - y dreams _ just slip through our _____ hands. _

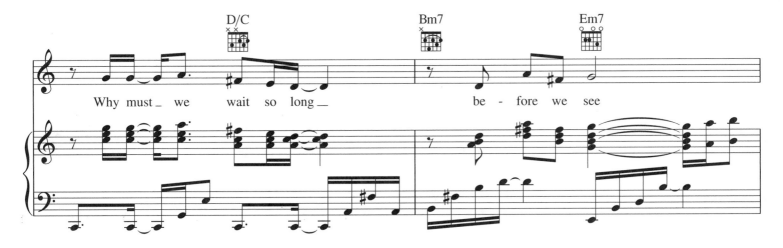

Why must__ we wait so long__ be - fore we see

D.S. al Coda

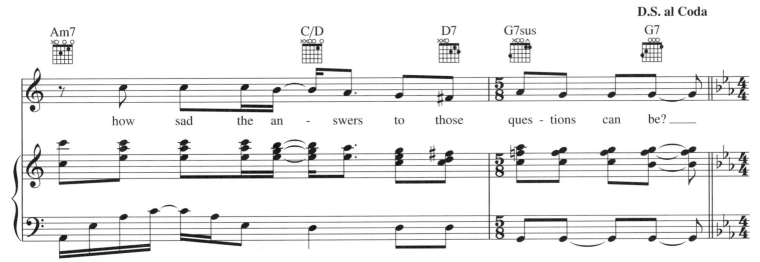

how sad the an - swers to those ques - tions can be?____

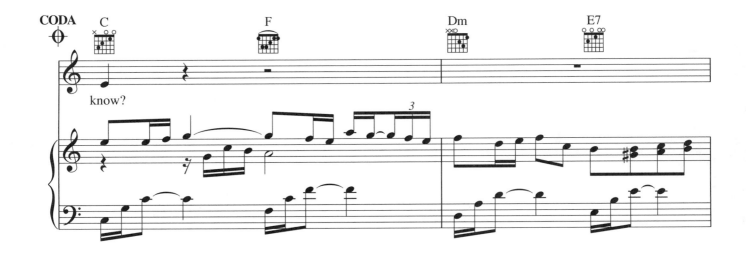

CODA

know?

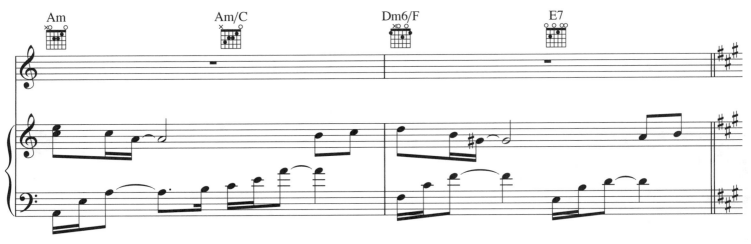

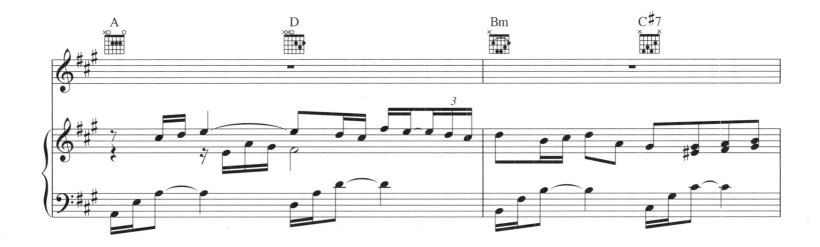

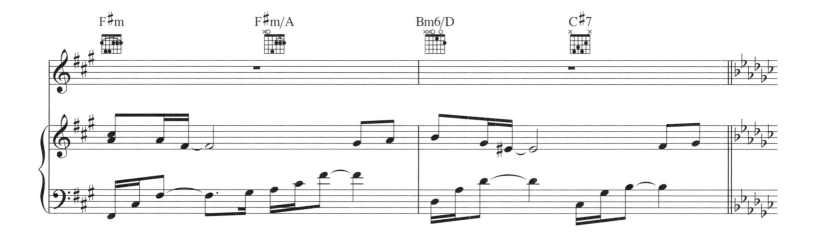

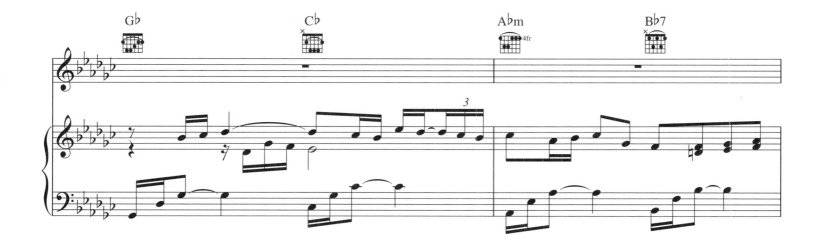

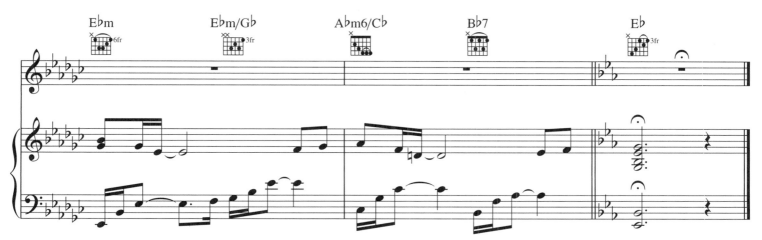

Emily

from the MGM Motion Picture THE AMERICANIZATION OF EMILY

Words by Johnny Mercer

Music by Johnny Mandel

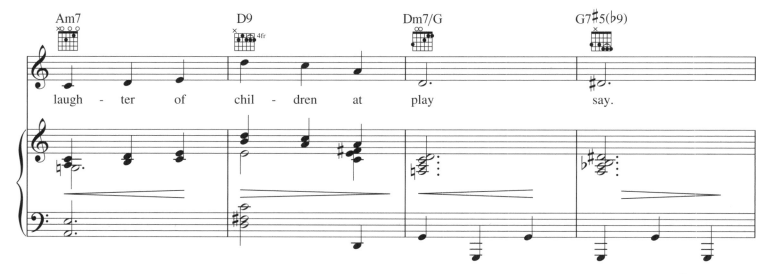

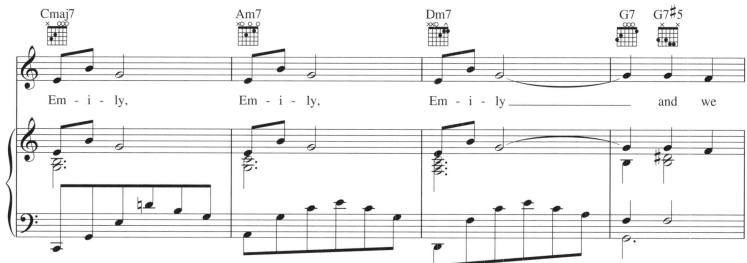

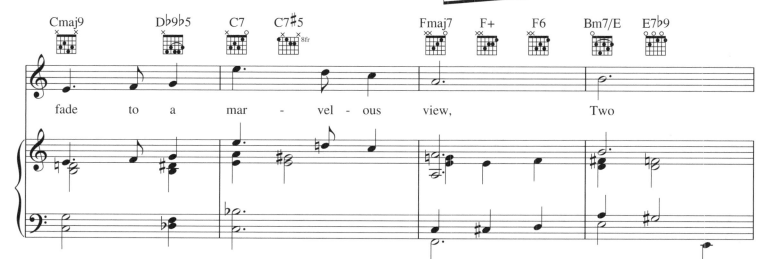

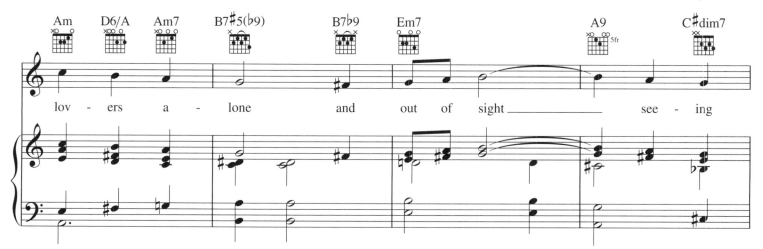

Endless Love

from ENDLESS LOVE

Words and Music by
Lionel Richie

64

they tell me how much you ___ care. _____ Oh, _____
you mean the world to ___ me. _____ Oh,

___ yes, you will al - ways be
I know I've found ____ in you

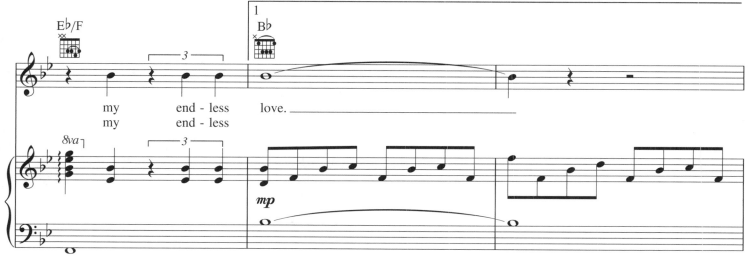

my end - less love. _____
my end - less

love. _____

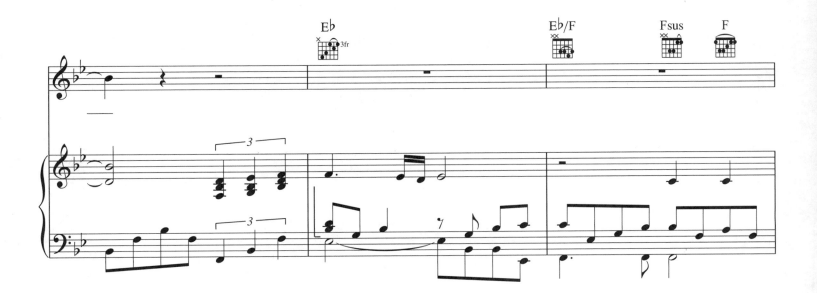

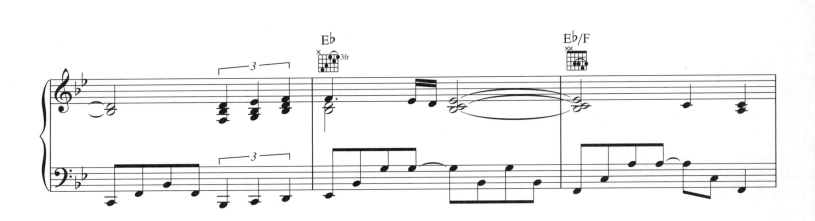

Oh, _____ and _ love, _____

this love _____ I have in - side.   I'll

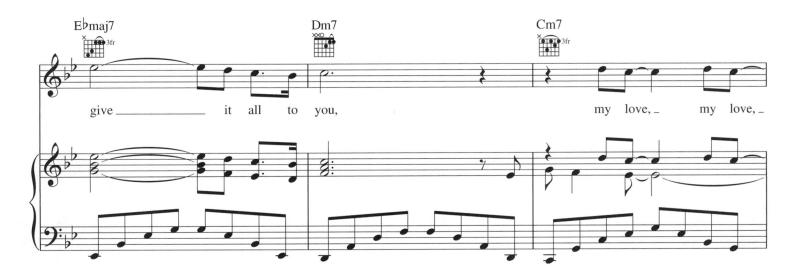

give _____ it all to you,   my love, _ my love, _

_____ my end - less love.

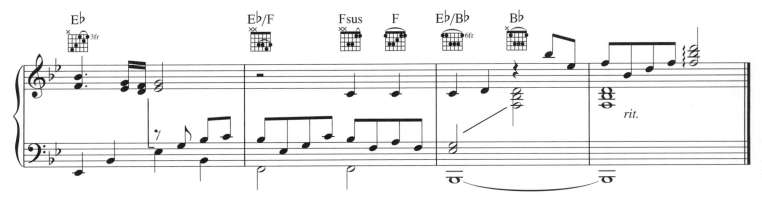

rit.

Everybody's Talkin'

(Echoes)

from MIDNIGHT COWBOY

Words and Music by
Fred Neil

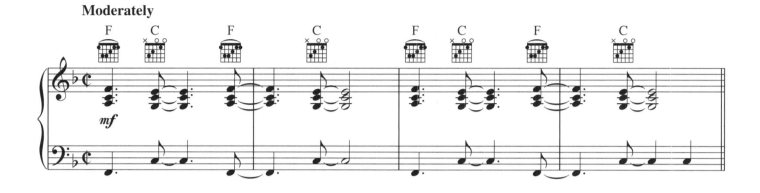

Ev - 'ry - bod - y's talk - in' at me, I don't hear a

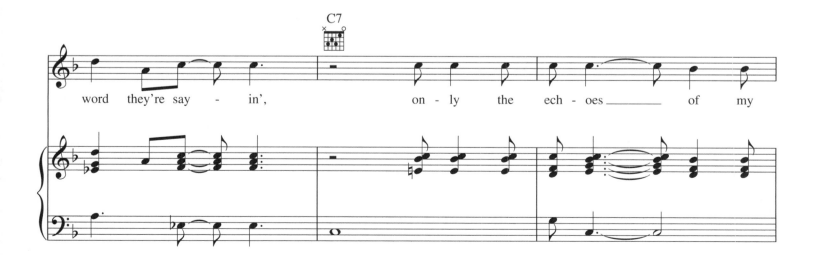

word they're say - in', on - ly the ech - oes of my

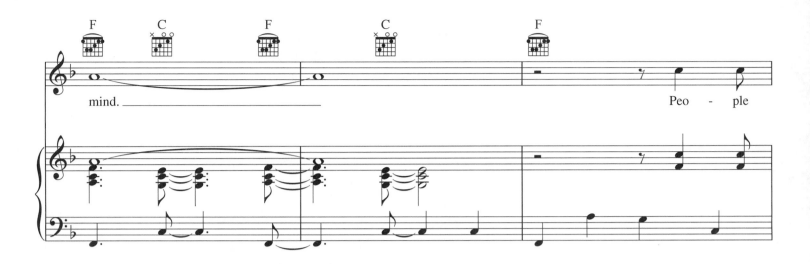

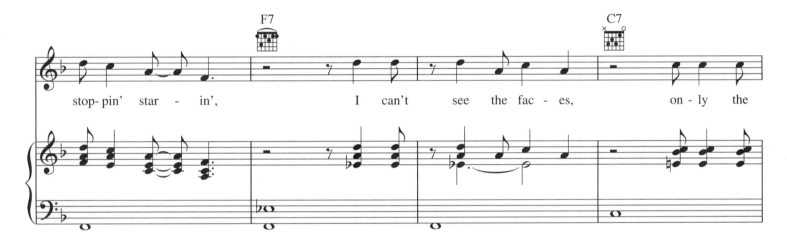

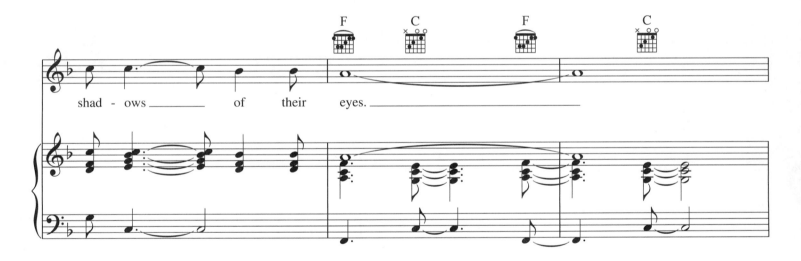

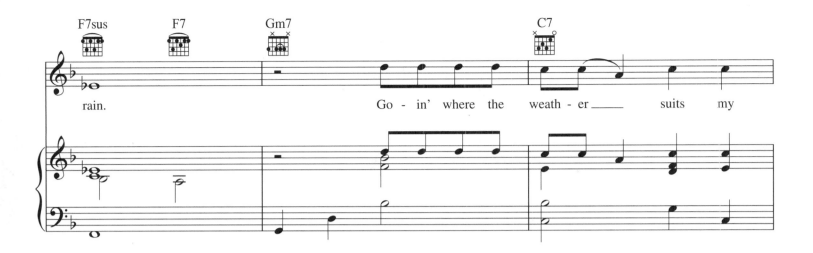

rain. Go - in' where the weath - er ____ suits my

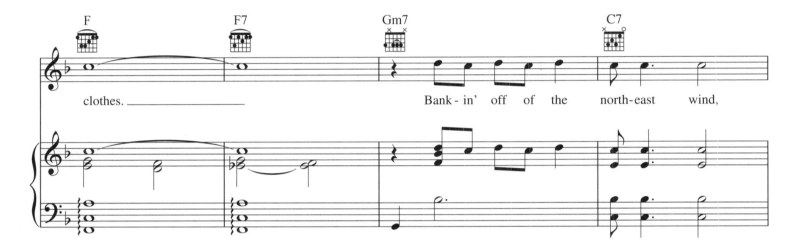

clothes. _____ Bank - in' off of the north-east wind,

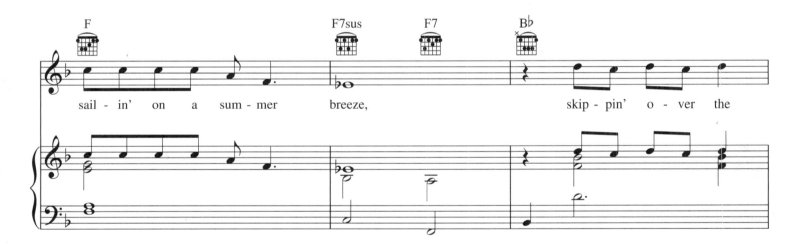

sail - in' on a sum - mer breeze, skip - pin' o - ver the

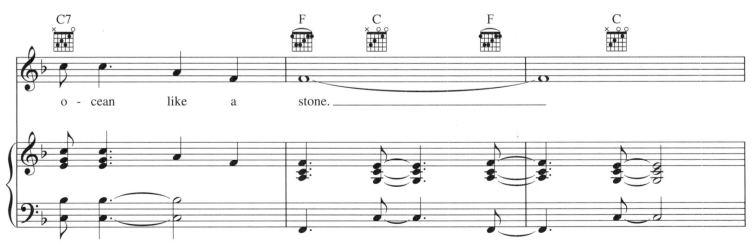

o - cean like a stone. _____

Ev-'ry-bod-y's talk-in' at me, I don't hear a

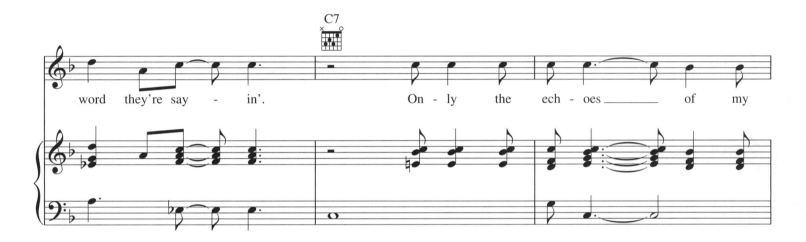

word they're say - in'. On - ly the ech - oes _____ of my

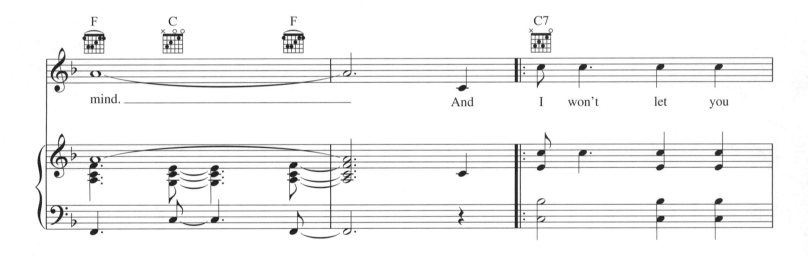

mind. _____ And I won't let you

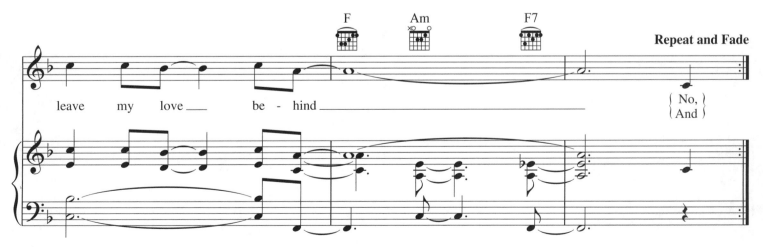

leave my love ____ be-hind _____

Repeat and Fade

{ No, }
{ And }

72

(Everything I Do)
I Do It For You

from the Motion Picture ROBIN HOOD: PRINCE OF THIEVES

Words and Music by
Bryan Adams, R.J. Lange
and Michael Kamen

74

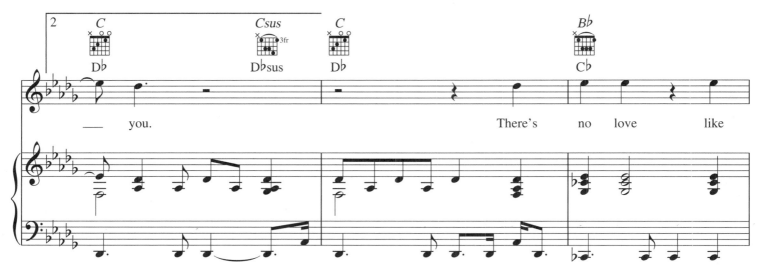

you. There's no love like

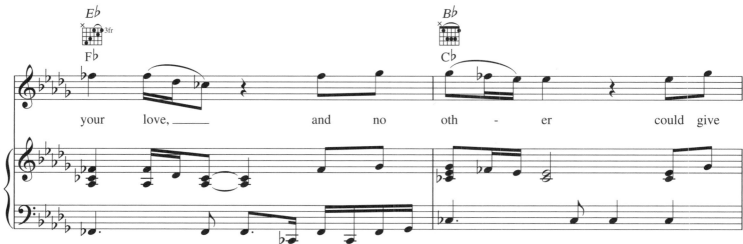

your love, _____ and no oth - er could give

more _____ love. There's no _____ way, _____ un - less

you're _____ there all the time, _____ all the

way, __ yeah. __

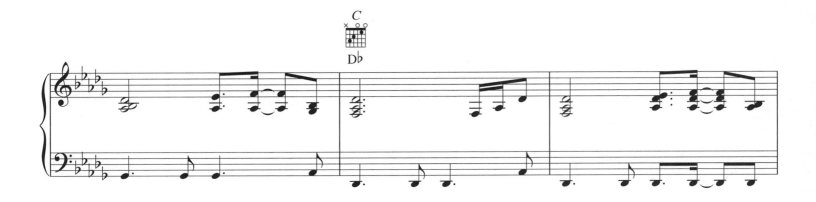

Oh, you can't tell me it's not worth try - ing for. I can't

76

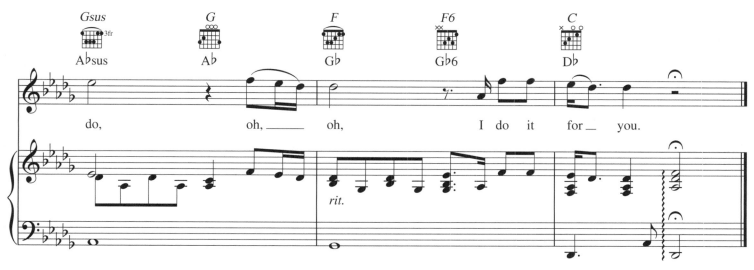

Exhale

(Shoop Shoop)

from the Original Soundtrack Album WAITING TO EXHALE

Words and Music by
Babyface

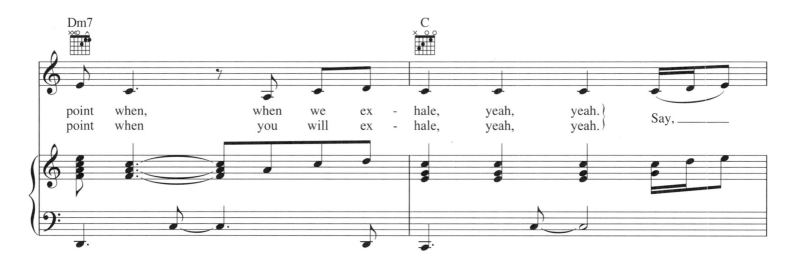

point when,   when we ex - hale, yeah,   yeah. }
point when   you will ex - hale, yeah,   yeah. }

Say, _____

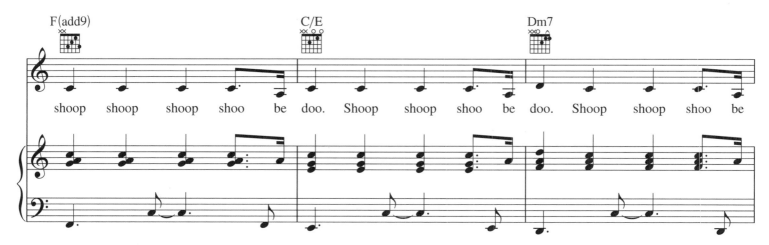

shoop shoop shoop shoo be doo. Shoop shoop shoo be doo. Shoop shoop shoo be

doo. Shoop shoop shoo be doo. Shoop shoop shoo be doo. Shoop shoop shoo be

doo. Shoop shoop shoo be doo.   Some - times you'll doo.

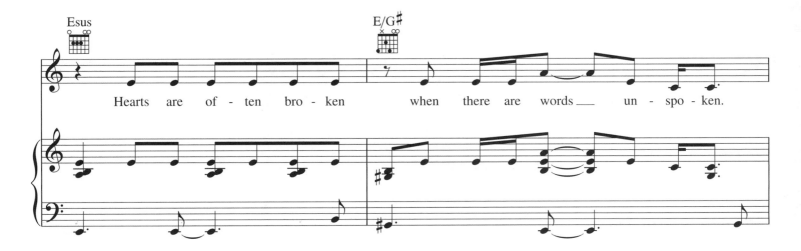

Hearts are of-ten bro-ken when there are words ___ un - spo - ken.

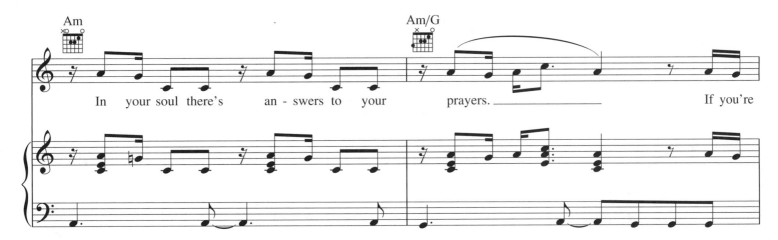

In your soul there's an-swers to your prayers. ___ If you're

search-ing for a place you know, a fa - mil - iar face, some-where to go, ___ you should

look in - side your soul, you're half-way there. ___ Some - times you'll

D.S. al Coda

CODA

doo.

Falling Slowly

from the Motion Picture ONCE

Words and Music by
Glen Hansard and Marketa Irglova

Slowly ♩ = 69

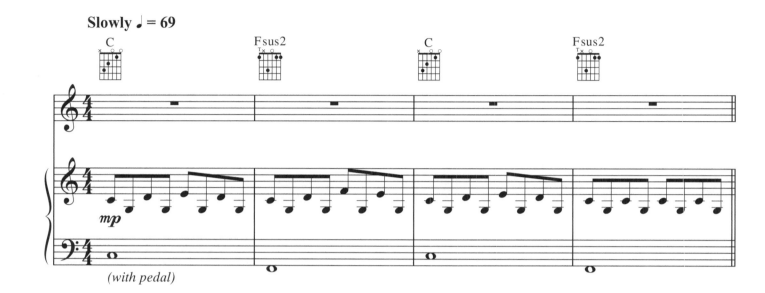

(with pedal)

Verse 1:

1. I don't know you, but I want you all the more for that.

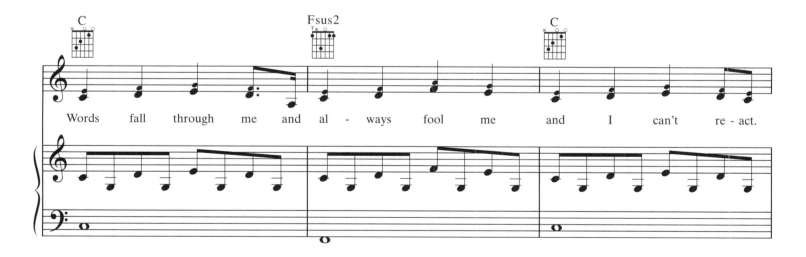

Words fall through me and al - ways fool me and I can't re - act.

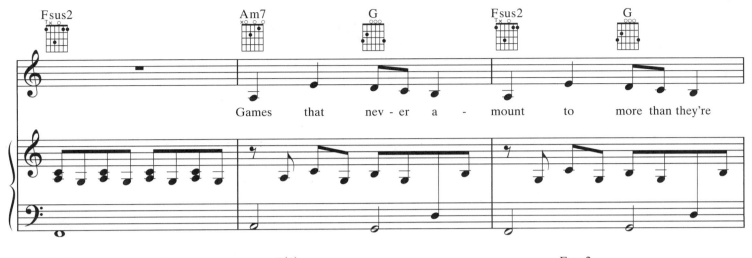

Games that nev-er a - mount to more than they're

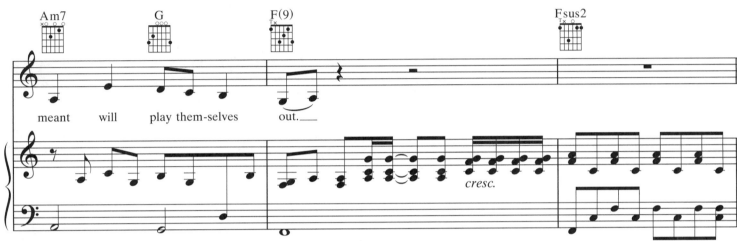

meant will play them-selves out.

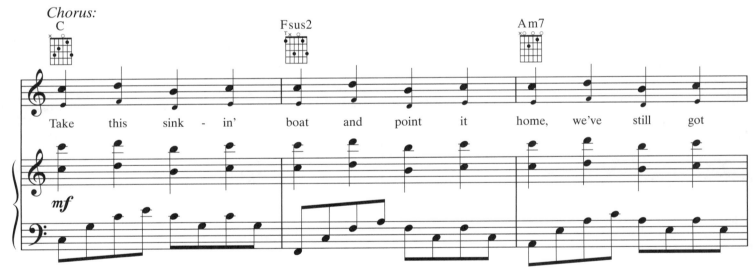

Chorus:

Take this sink - in' boat and point it home, we've still got

time. Raise your hope - ful voice, you have a

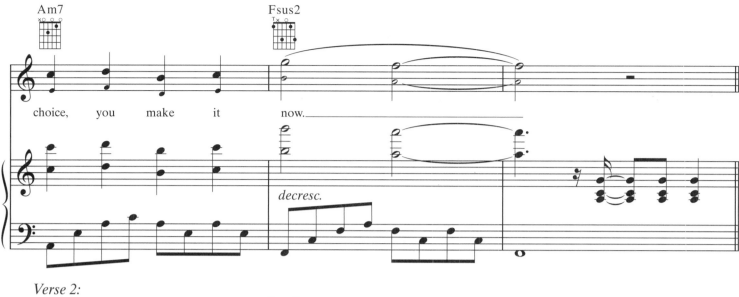

choice, you make it now.

Verse 2:

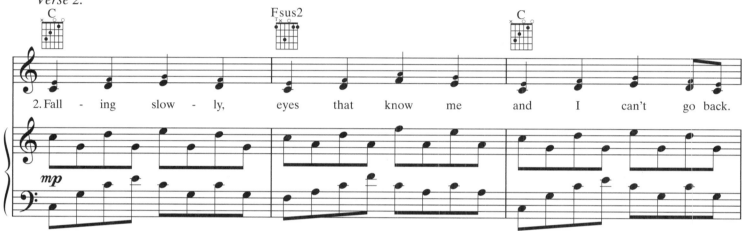

2. Fall - ing slow - ly, eyes that know me and I can't go back.

Moods that take me and e - rase me and I'm paint - ed black.

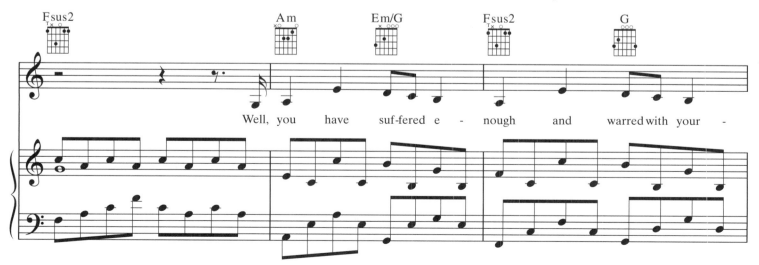

Well, you have suf - fered e - nough and warred with your -

sing your mel - o - dy, I'll sing it loud.

(Strings)

Take it all.

I paid the cost_____ too late,_____

now you're gone._

85

(Strings)

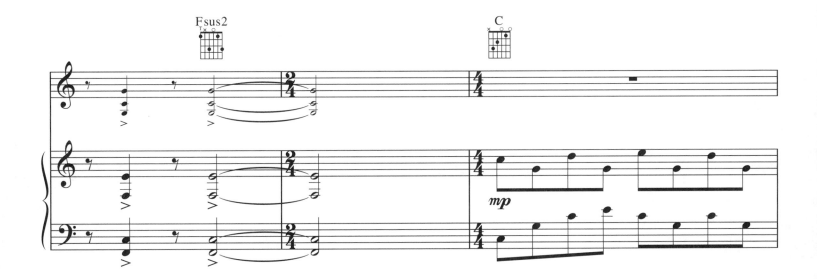

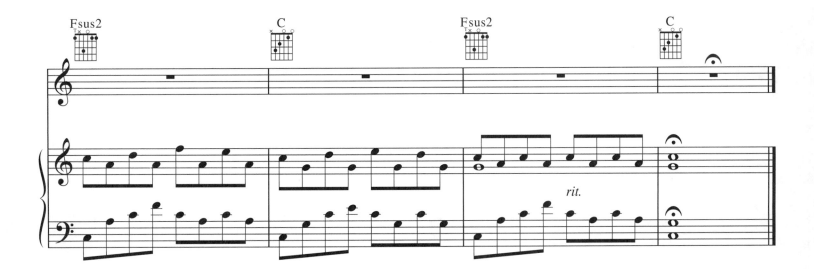

For All We Know

from the Motion Picture LOVERS AND OTHER STRANGERS

Words by
Robb Wilson and Arthur James

Music by Fred Karlin

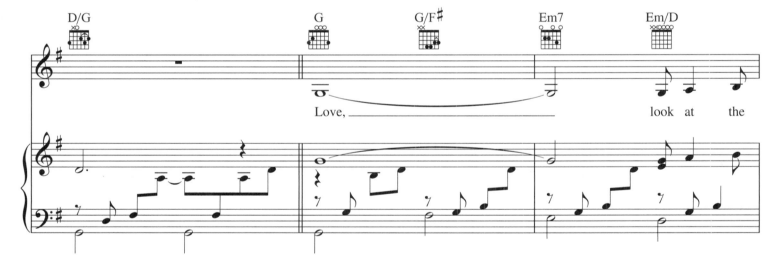

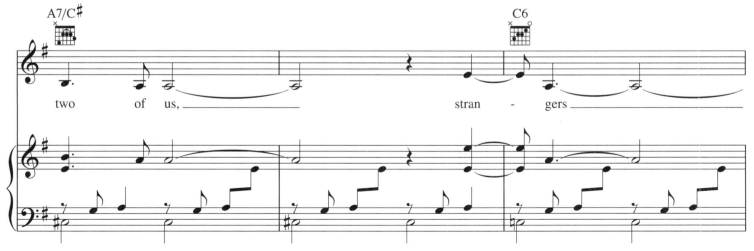

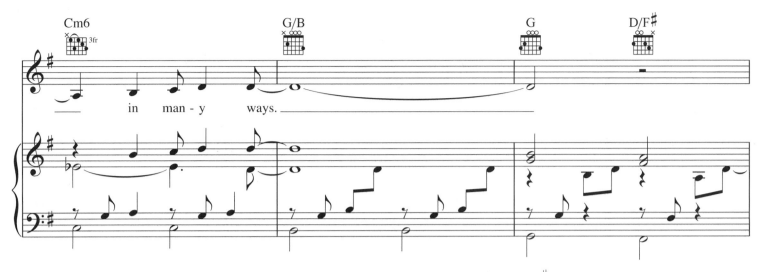

in man-y ways.

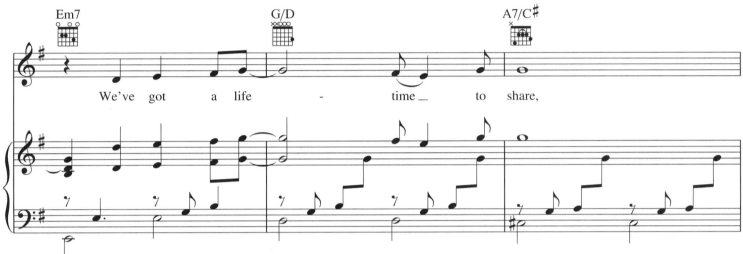

We've got a life - time to share,

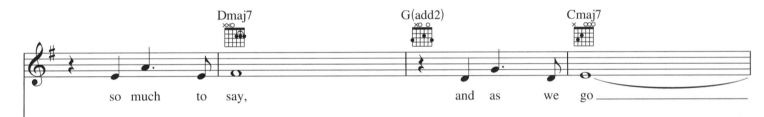

so much to say, and as we go

from day to day, I'll feel you

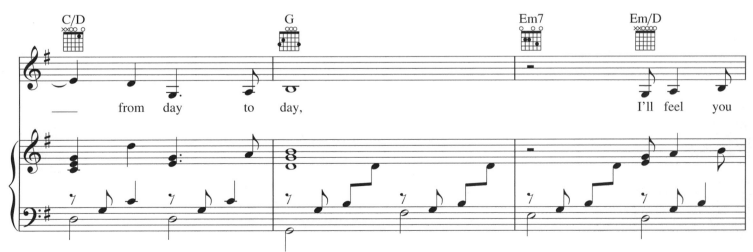

and love may grow, for all ____ we

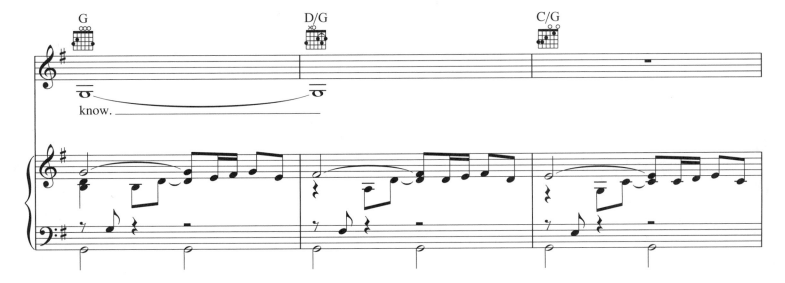

know. ____

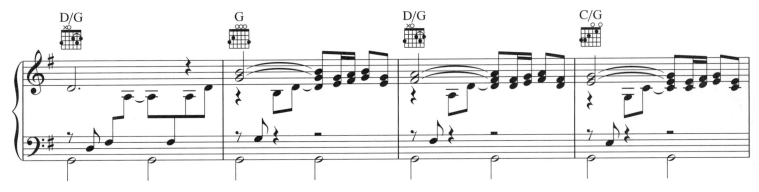

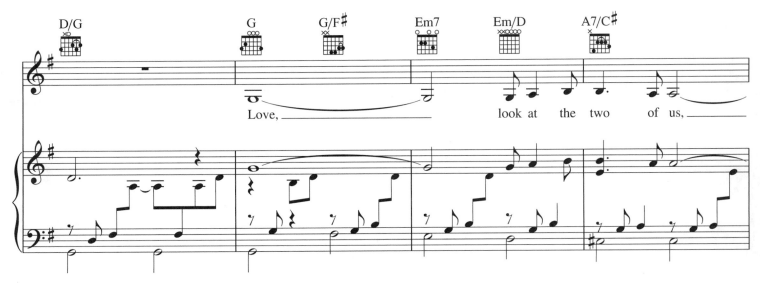

Love, ____ look at the two of us, ____

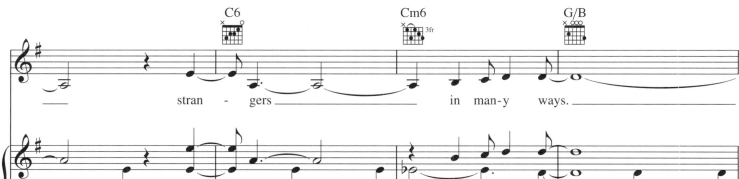

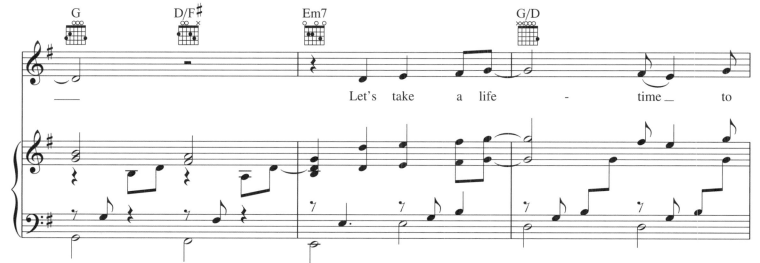

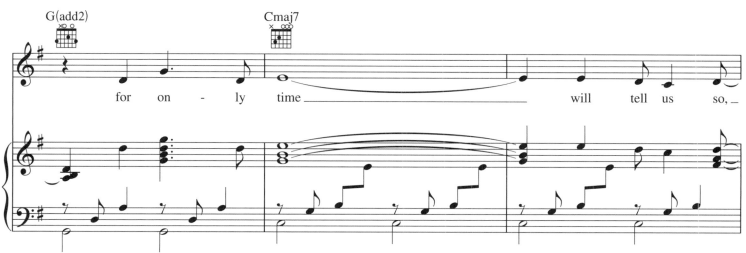

and love may grow, for all ____ we

know. _____

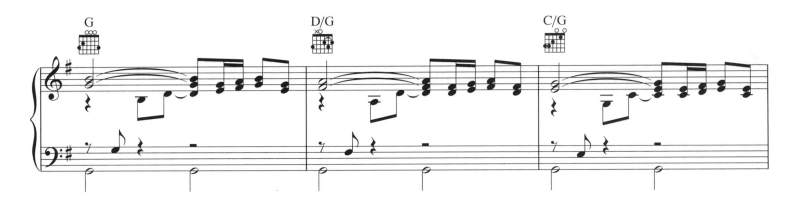

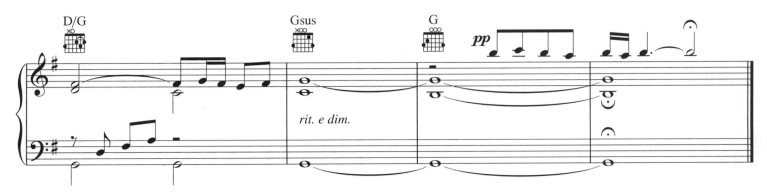

rit. e dim.

pp

From Here to Eternity

from FROM HERE TO ETERNITY

Words by Robert Wells

Music by Fred Karger

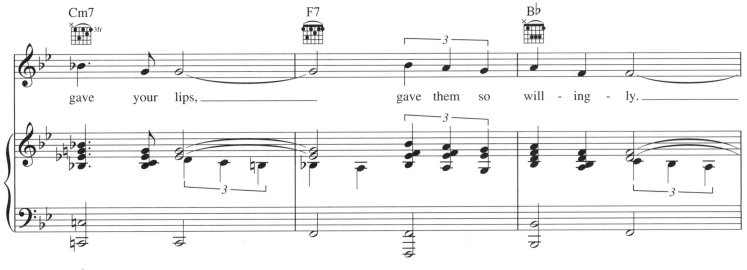

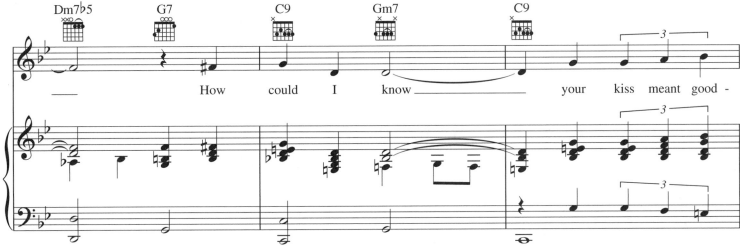

94

Glory of Love

Theme from KARATE KID PART II

Words and Music by
David Foster, Peter Cetera
and Diane Nini

To - night it's ver - y clear, as we're both stand - ing here,

there's so man - y things I want to say.

I will al-ways love you, ____   I will nev-er leave you ____ a - lone. ____

Some-times I just for - get,   say things I might re - gret, ____
You keep me stand - ing tall,   you help me through it all, ____

it breaks my heart ____ to see ____ you cry - ing.
I'm al - ways strong ____ when you're ____ be - side   me.

- ry of love.

Just like a knight in shin-ing ar - mor, from a long time a-go,

just in time I will save the day, _ take you to my cas-tle far a - way. _

We'll live for-ev - er, know-ing to-geth - er that we did it all __ for the glo-

- ry of love. __ We did __ it all __ for love. __

We did __ it all __ for love. __

Repeat and Fade

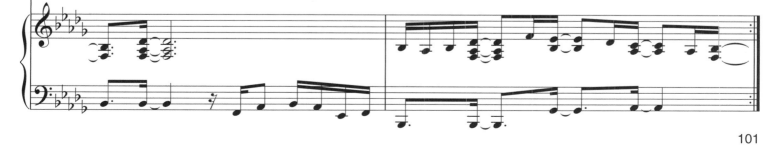

We did __ it all __ for love. __

The Godfather

(Love Theme)

from the Paramount Picture THE GODFATHER

By Nino Rota

Slowly and expressively

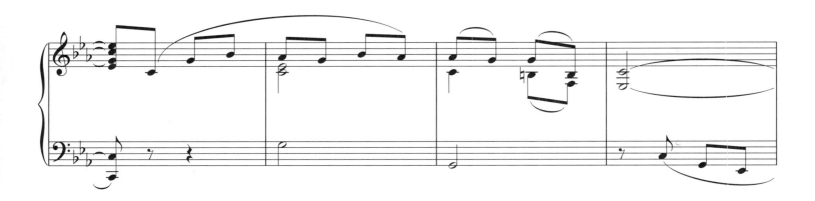

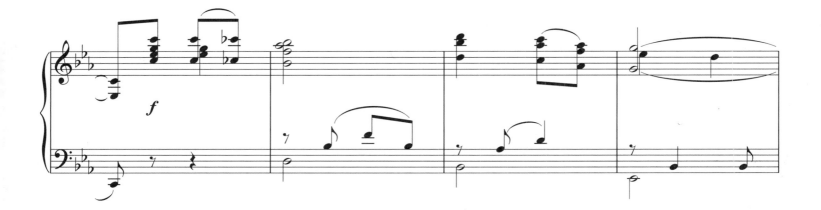

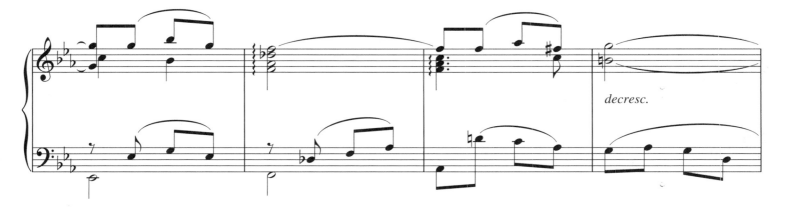

104

Goldfinger

from GOLDFINGER

Lyrics by
Leslie Bricusse and Anthony Newley

Music by John Barry

beck-ons you   to   en - ter   his   web   of

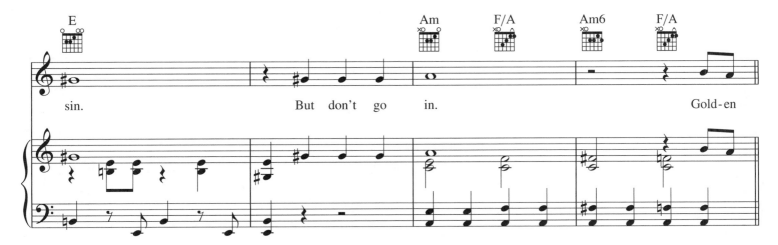

sin.   But   don't   go   in.   Gold-en

words   he   will   pour   in   your   ear,   but   his   lies   can't   dis - guise   what   you

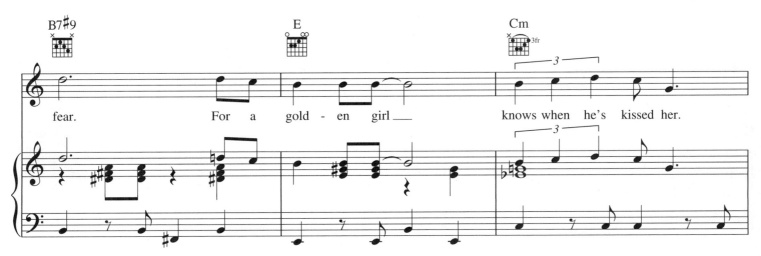

fear.   For   a   gold - en   girl ___   knows   when   he's   kissed   her.

It's the kiss of death from Mis - ter Gold - fin - ger.

Pret - ty girl, be - ware of this heart of

gold.   This heart is cold.

Gold - en cold.   He loves on - ly

107

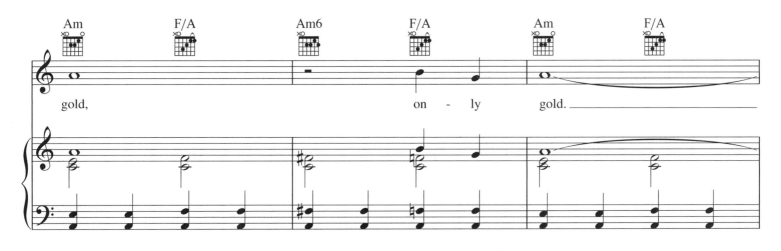

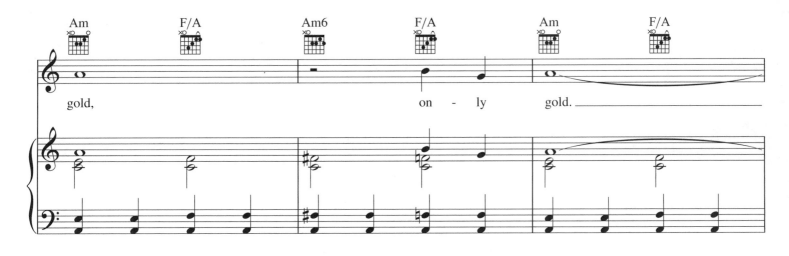

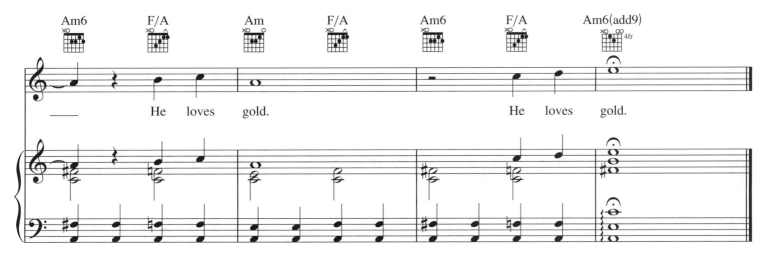

Gonna Fly Now

Theme from ROCKY

By Bill Conti,
Ayn Robbins and Carol Connors

try - in' hard   now, _____   Rock - y   pow - er _____   by the
get - tin' strong now, _____   fists like thun - der _____   gon - na put you

hour,   pump-in' i - ron _____   God ya know he's   try - in'. _____
un - der, _____   pump-in' i - ron _____   God ya know I'm   try - in'. _____

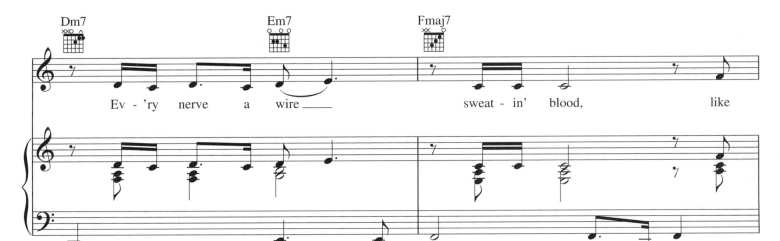

Ev - 'ry nerve a wire _____   sweat - in' blood,   like

fire. _____   Gon - na

fly now, _____ fly-ing high now. _____

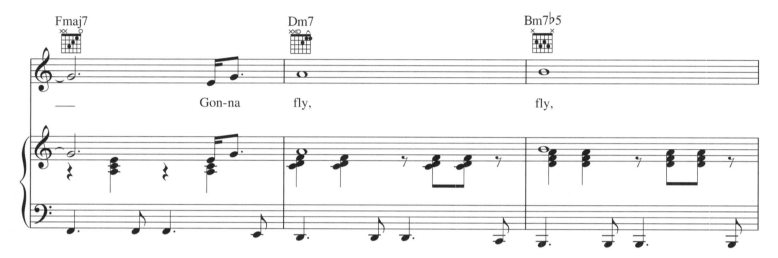

Gon-na fly, fly,

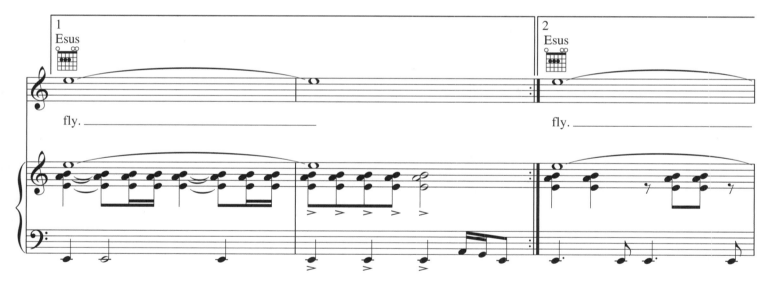

fly. _____ fly. _____

Happy Days Are Here Again

from CHASING RAINBOWS

Words by
Jack Yellen

Music by
Milton Ager

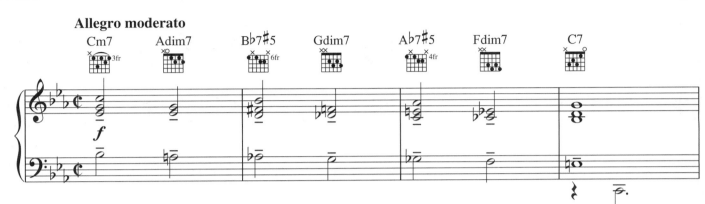

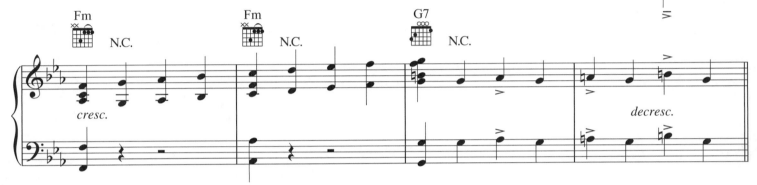

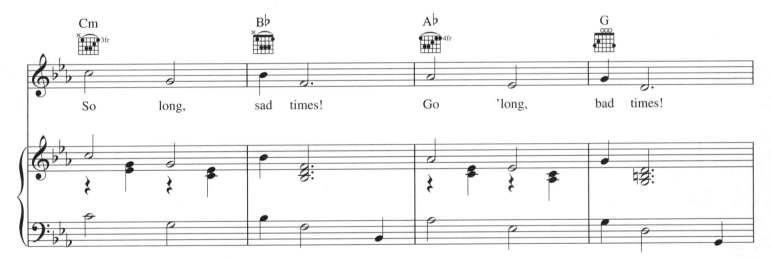

So long, sad times! Go 'long, bad times!

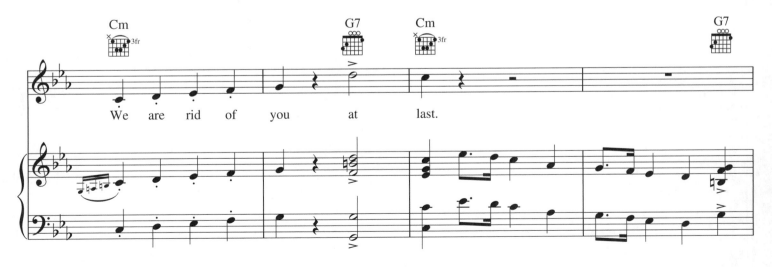

We are rid of you at last.

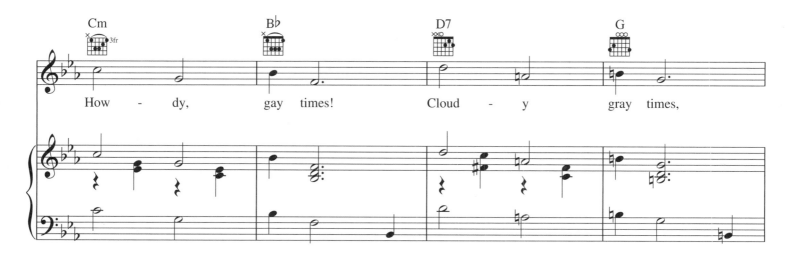

How - dy, gay times! Cloud - y gray times,

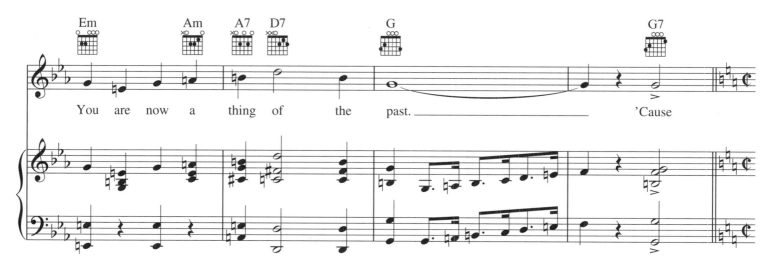

You are now a thing of the past. _____ 'Cause

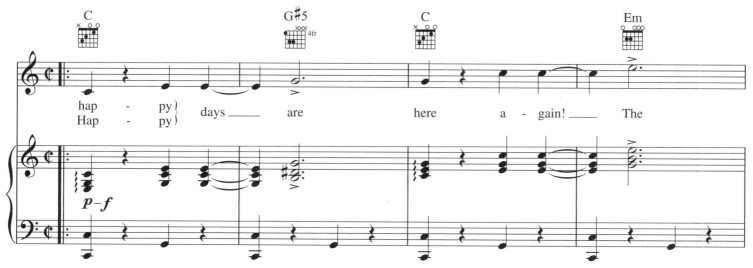

hap - py } days _____ are here a - gain! _____ The
Hap - py }

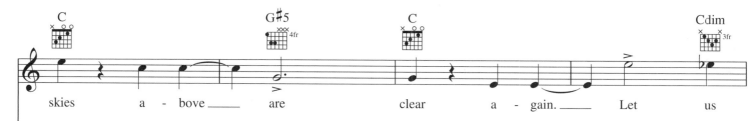

skies a - bove _____ are clear a - gain. _____ Let us

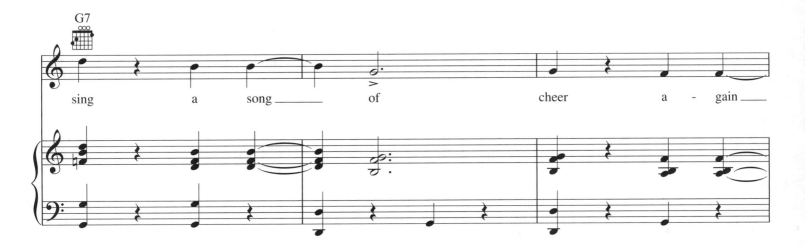

sing   a   song _____ of   cheer   a - gain _____

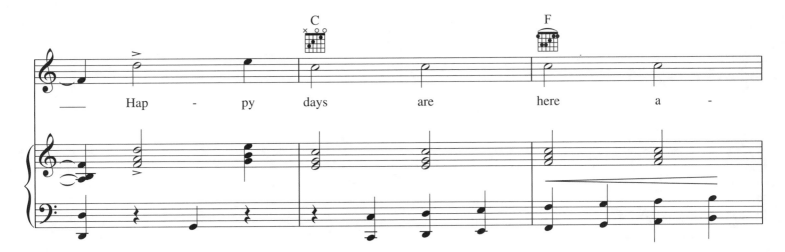

_____ Hap - py days   are   here   a -

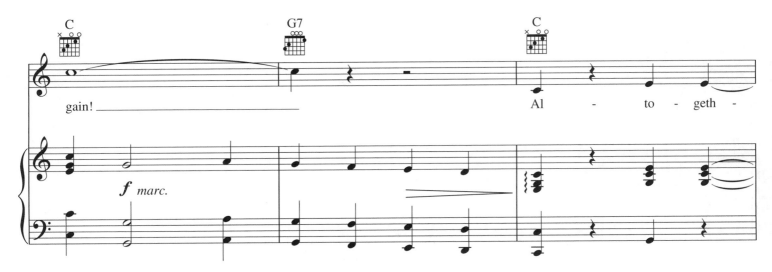

gain! _____   Al - to - geth -

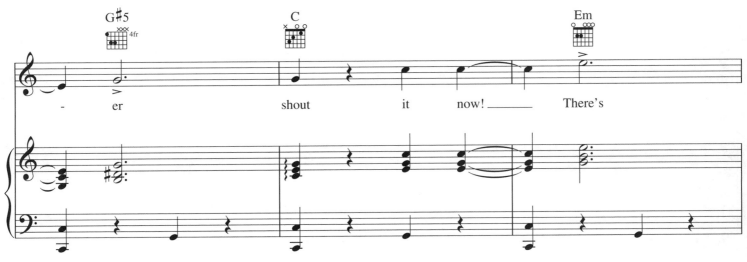

- er   shout   it   now! _____ There's

116

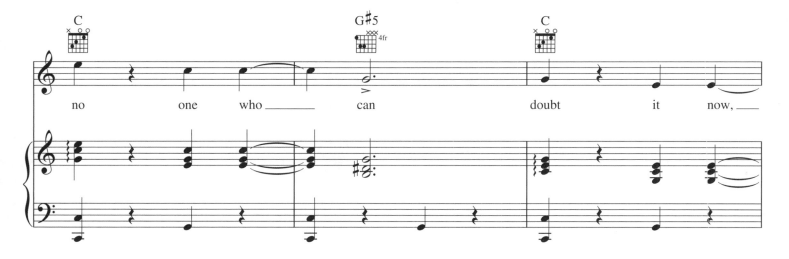

no one who ____ can doubt it now, ____

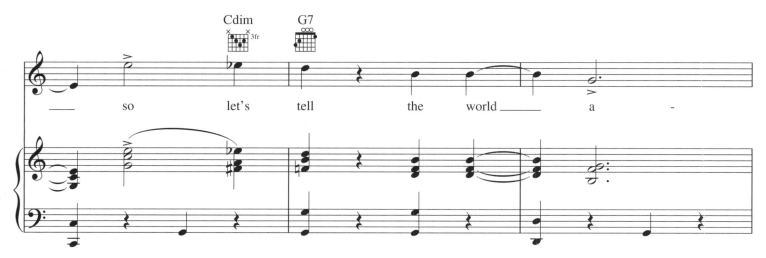

____ so let's tell the world a -

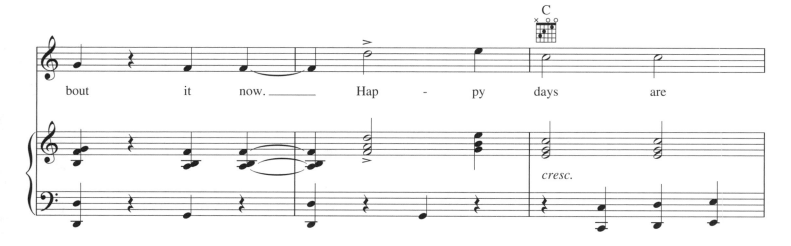

bout it now. ____ Hap - py days are

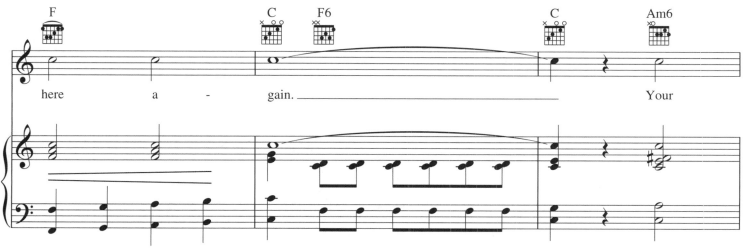

here a - gain. ____ Your

117

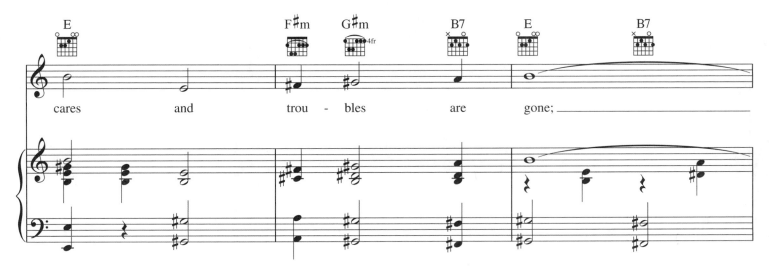

cares and trou - bles are gone; _____

____ There'll be no more from now

on. _____ Hap - py days ____

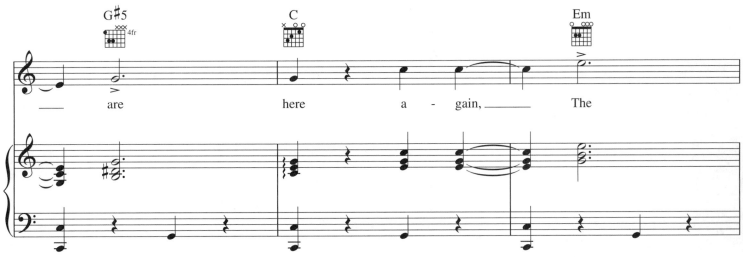

____ are here a - gain, _____ The

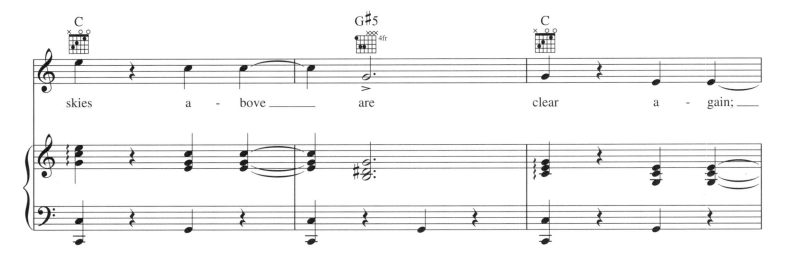

skies a - bove _____ are clear a - gain; _____

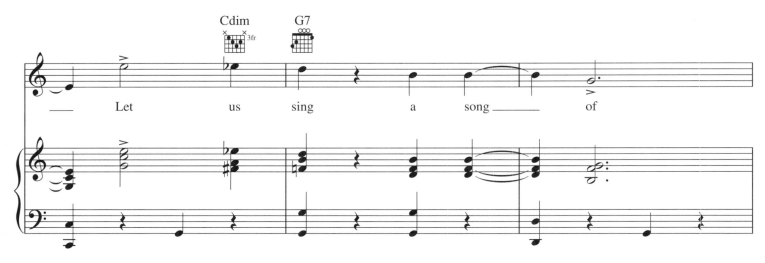

_____ Let us sing a song _____ of

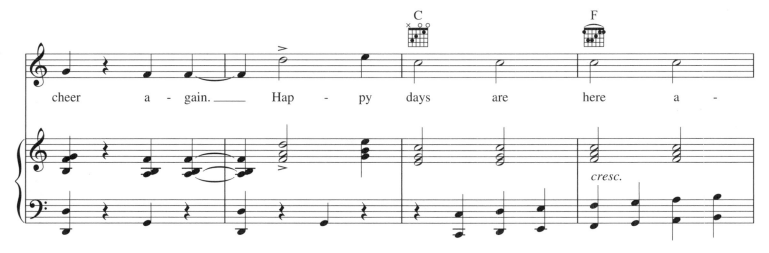

cheer a - gain. _____ Hap - py days are here a -

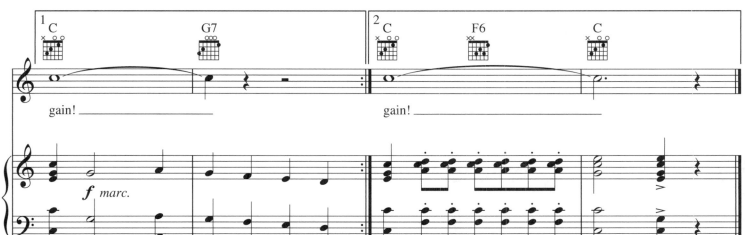

gain! _____ gain! _____

A Hard Day's Night

from A HARD DAY'S NIGHT

Words and Music by
John Lennon and Paul McCartney

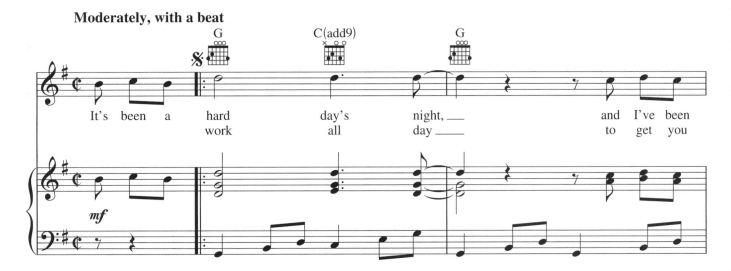

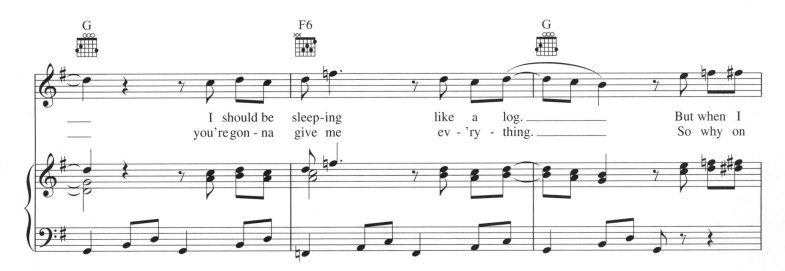

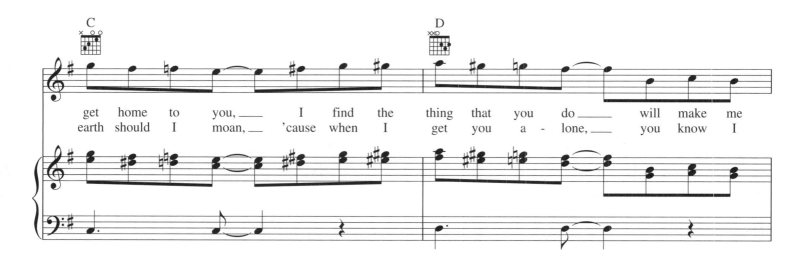

get home to you, ____ I find the thing that you do ____ will make me

earth should I moan, ____ 'cause when I get you a - lone, ____ you know I

feel __ al - right. ____

feel __ O - K. ____

You know, I

When I'm home, __

____

ev - 'ry - thing seems __ to be ____ right.

When I'm home, ___

feel - ing you hold - ing me

tight,   tight, yeah. It's been a hard day's night, —

— and I've been work-ing like a dog. —— It's been a

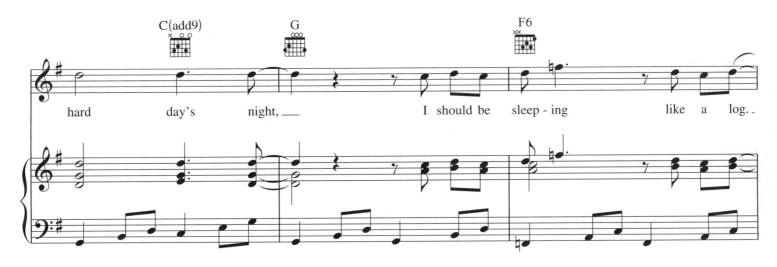

hard day's night, — I should be sleep-ing like a log.

—— But when I get home to you, — I find the thing that you do — will make me

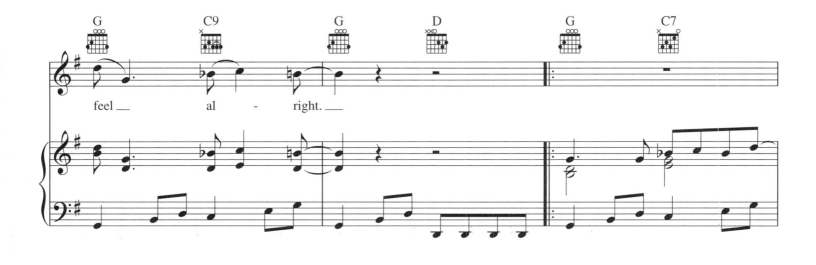

feel __ al - right. __

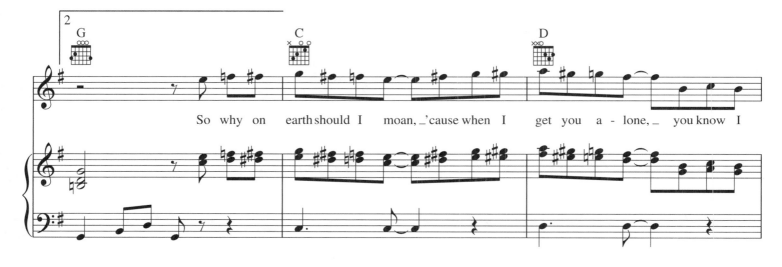

So why on earth should I moan, _'cause when I get you a - lone, _ you know I

feel __ O - K. ____ When I'm home, __

123

ev -'ry-thing seems _ to be al - right.   When I'm   home, _

feel - ing you hold - ing me tight,   tight,   yeah.   It's been a

D.S. al Coda
(Verse 1)

You know I feel _ al - right. _   You know I

Repeat and Fade

feel   al - right. _

124

High Hopes

from A HOLE IN THE HEAD

Words by Sammy Cahn

Music by James Van Heusen

Next time you're found __ with your chin on the ground, __ there's a
When trou - bles call __ and your back's to the wall, __ there's a

Instrumental...

lot to be learned, __ so look a - round. _____
lot to be learned; __ that wall could fall. _____

Just what makes that lit - tle ol' ant __ think he'll move that
Once there was a sil - ly ol' ram, __ thought he'd punch a

rub - ber tree plant. ___ An - y - one knows ___ an ant can't ___
hole in a dam. ___ No one could make ___ that ram scram; ___

move a rub - ber tree plant. But he's got high ___ hopes, he's got
he kept butt - in' that dam, 'cause he had high ___ hopes, he had
...Instrumental ends So keep your high ___ hopes, keep your

high ___ hopes, he's got high ap - ple pie in the
high ___ hopes, he had high ap - ple pie in the
high ___ hopes, keep those high ap - ple pie in the

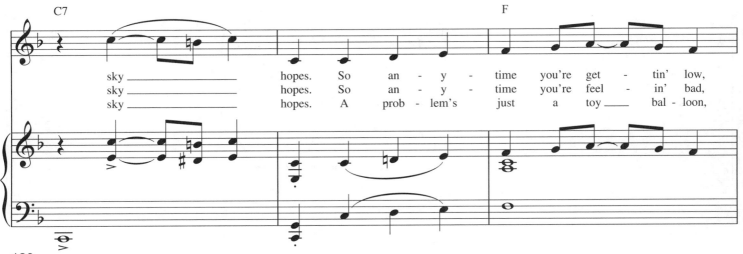

sky ___ hopes. So an - y - time you're get - tin' low,
sky ___ hopes. So an - y - time you're feel - in' bad,
sky ___ hopes. A prob - lem's just a toy ___ bal - loon,

'stead of let - tin' go, just re - mem - ber that ant.
'stead of feel - in' sad, just re - mem - ber that ram.
they'll be burst - ing soon, they're just bound to go, "Pop!"

(Oops! There goes an -
(Oops! There goes a
(Oops! There goes an -

Oops! There goes an - oth - er rub - ber tree plant.
Oops! There goes a bil - lion kil - o - watt dam.
Oops! There goes an - oth - er prob - lem, ker - plop!

oth - er rub - ber tree plant.)
bil - lion kil - o - watt dam.)
oth - er prob - lem, ker - plop!)

Oops! There goes an - oth - er rub - ber tree
Oops! There goes a bil - lion kil - o - watt
Oops! There goes an - oth - er prob - lem, ker -

plant.
dam.

plop! Ker - plop!

I Don't Want to Miss a Thing

from the Touchstone Picture ARMAGEDDON

Words and Music by
Diane Warren

smile while you are sleep - ing,___ while you're far a - way___ and dream - ing. I could

spend my life___ in this sweet sur - ren - der. I could stay lost in this mo - ment for -

ev - er. Ev - 'ry mo - ment spent with you___ is a mo - ment I trea - sure.

§ Chorus:

Don't wan - na close___ my eyes,___ don't wan - na fall___ a - sleep,___ 'coz I'd

miss you, ba - by, and I don't wan-na miss a thing.___ 'Coz e - ven when I dream of you,___

the sweet-est dream would nev - er do.___ I'd still miss you, ba - by, and I don't wan-na miss a thing.___

2. Lay - ing

Verse 2:

close to you,___ feel - ing your___ heart beat - ing, and I'm

won-d'ring what you're dream-ing, won-d'ring if it's me you're see-ing. Then I

kiss your eyes___ and thank God we're to-geth - er.___ I just wan-na

stay with you___ in this mo-ment for-ev - er, for-ev - er and ev-er.___

Coda

I don't wan-na miss one smile;___ I don't wan-na

miss one kiss. I just wan-na be with you,___ right here___ with you,___

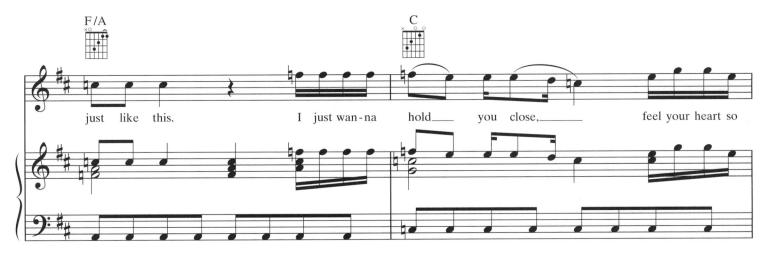

just like this. I just wan-na hold___ you close,_____ feel your heart so

close to mine,_____ and just stay here in___ this mo-ment for all the

rest of time.___ Ba - by, ba - by.___

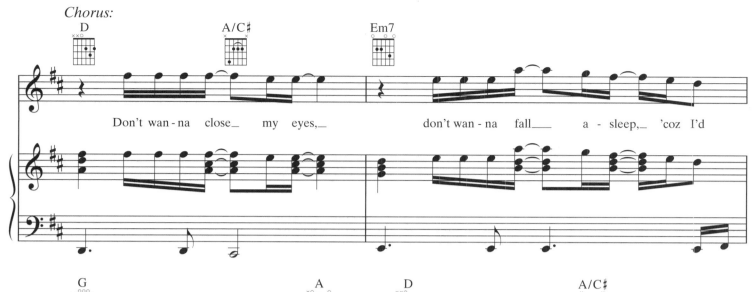

Chorus:

Don't wan - na close__ my eyes,__ don't wan - na fall__ a - sleep,__ 'coz I'd

miss you, ba - by, and I don't wan - na miss a thing.__ 'Coz e - ven when I dream of you,__

the sweet - est dream would nev - er do.__ I'd still miss you, ba - by, and I don't wan - na miss a thing.__

__ Don't wan - na close__ my eyes,__ don't wan - na fall__ a - sleep,__ 'coz I'd

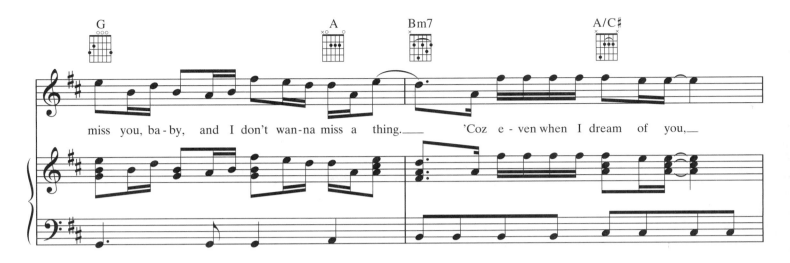

miss you, ba - by, and I don't wan-na miss a thing.___ 'Coz e - ven when I dream of you,___

the sweet-est dream would nev - er do.___ I'd still miss you, ba - by, and I don't wan-na miss a thing.___

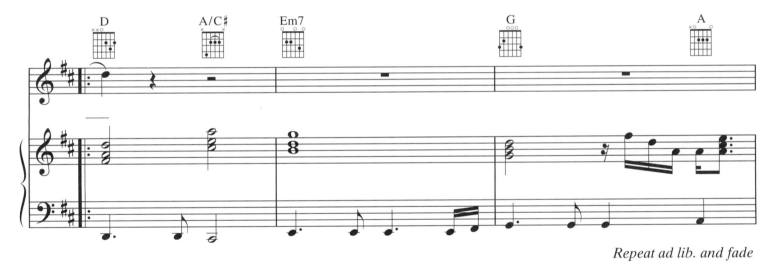

Repeat ad lib. and fade

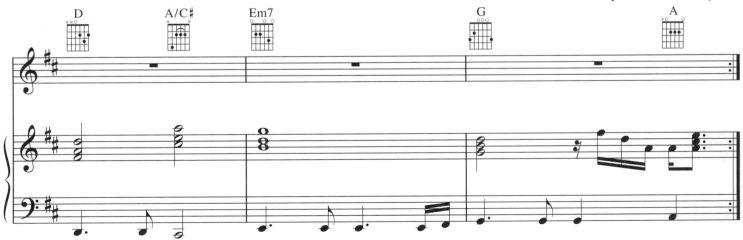

134

I Will Always Love You

featured in THE BODYGUARD

Words and Music by
Dolly Parton

will _ al - ways _ love _ you. _____ I _____

D.S.

_____ will _ al - ways _ love _ you. _____

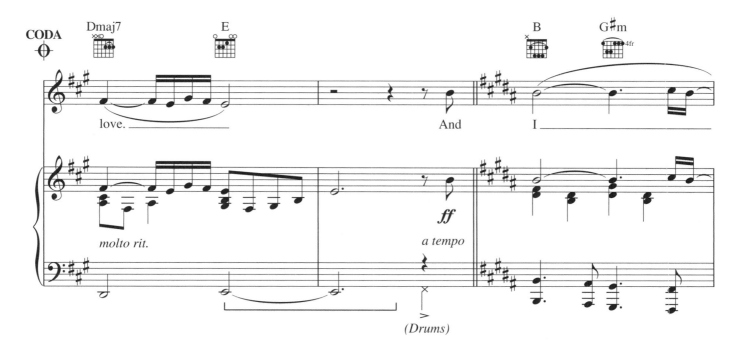

love. _____ And I _____

molto rit.

ff

a tempo

(Drums)

will al - ways love you. I will al - ways love

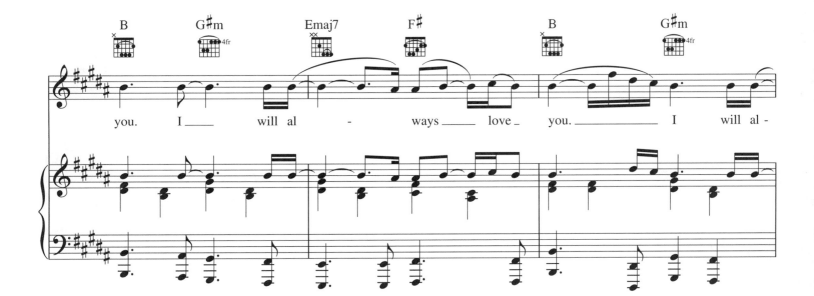

you. I will al - ways love you. I will al -

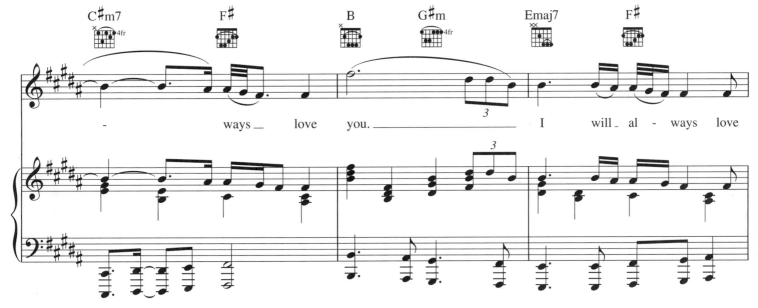

ways love you. I will al - ways love

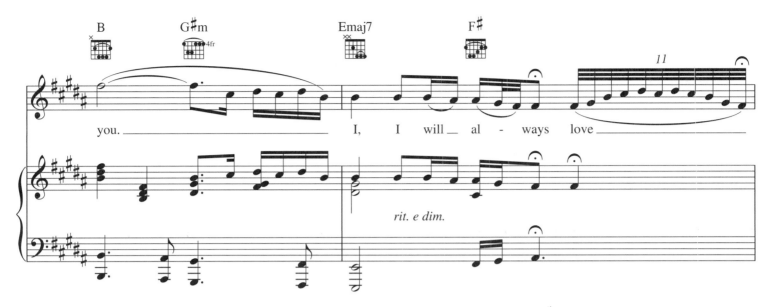

you. _____ I, I will __ al - ways love _____

rit. e dim.

you. _____ You, _____ dar - ling, I love _ you. Ooh, ___ I'll _

a tempo

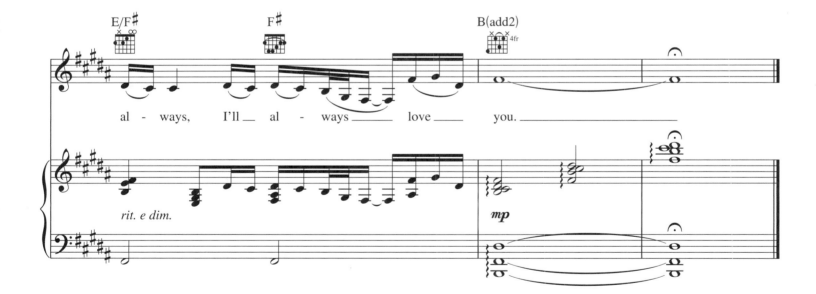

al - ways, I'll _ al - ways love ___ you. _____

rit. e dim.   *mp*

Additional Lyrics

3. I hope life treats you kind.
And I hope you have all you've dreamed of.
And I wish to you, joy and happiness.
But above all this, I wish you love.

I Will Remember You

Theme from THE BROTHERS McMULLEN

Words and Music by
Sarah McLachlan, Seamus Egan
and Dave Merenda

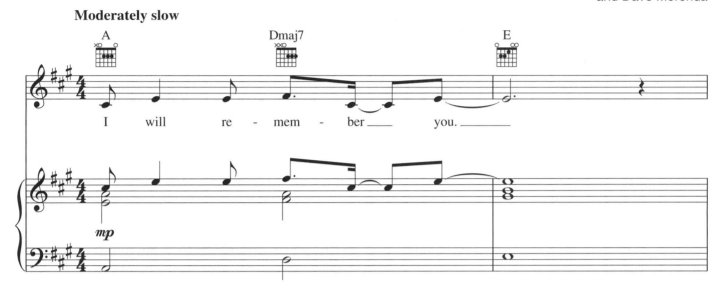

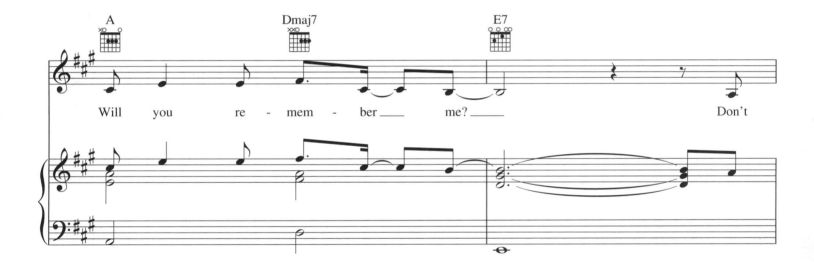

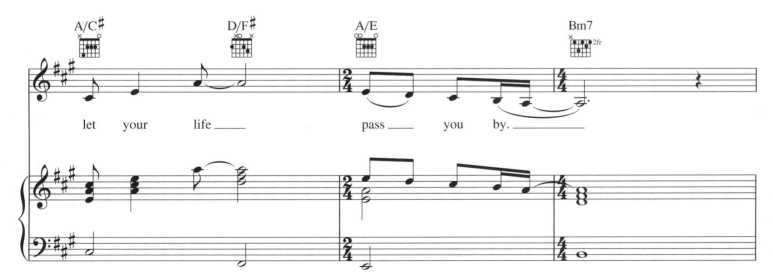

141

_____ your warmth up-on _____ me. I wan-na be the one. _____
ing in - side or we _____ can't be heard.
gave me ev-'ry-thing you had, oh, you gave me light. _____

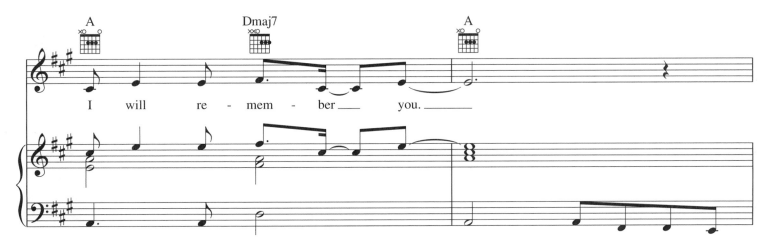

I will re-mem-ber _____ you. _____

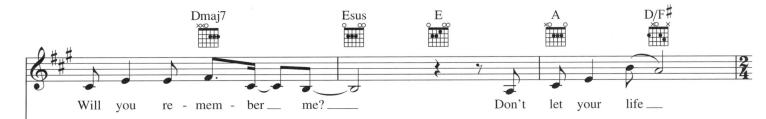

Will you re-mem-ber _____ me? _____ Don't let your life _____

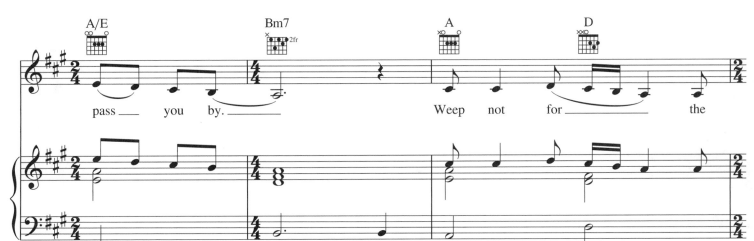

pass _____ you by. _____ Weep not for _____ the

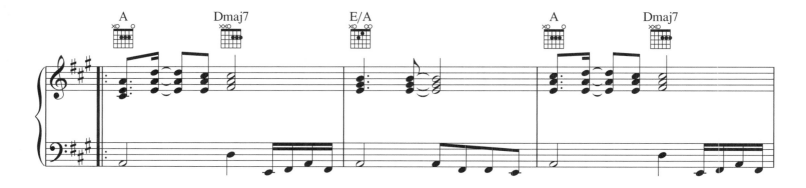

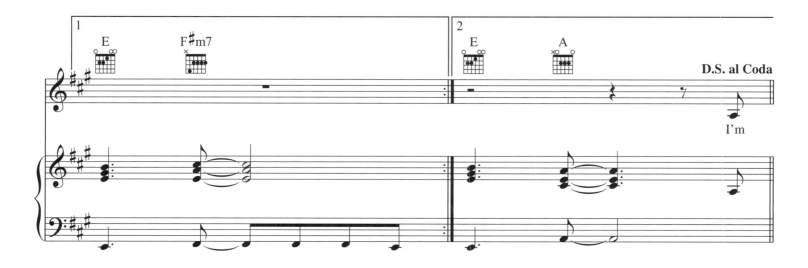

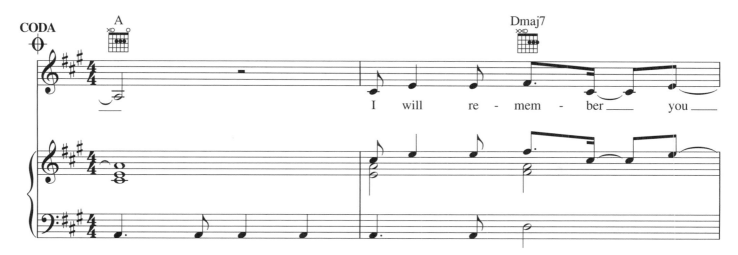

Will you re- mem - ber me? _____ Don't

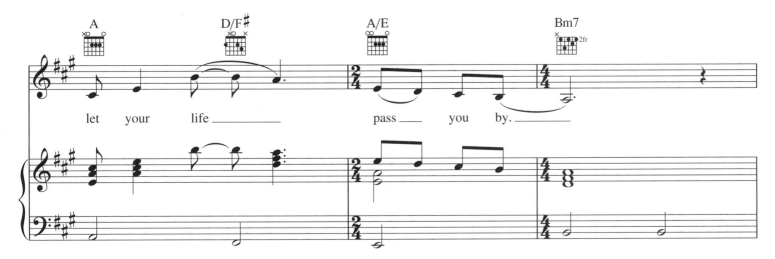

let your life _____ pass _____ you by. _____

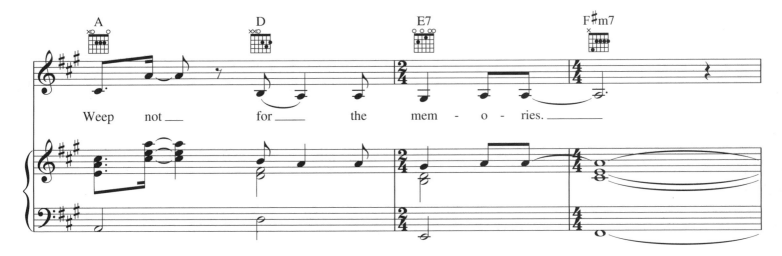

Weep not _____ for _____ the mem - o - ries. _____

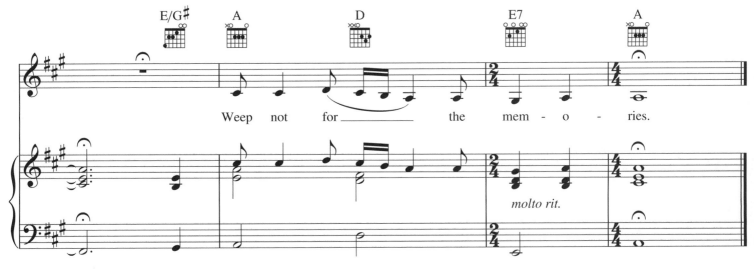

Weep not for _____ the mem - o - ries.

molto rit.

(I've Had)
The Time of My Life

from DIRTY DANCING

Words and Music by
Franke Previte, John DeNicola
and Donald Markowitz

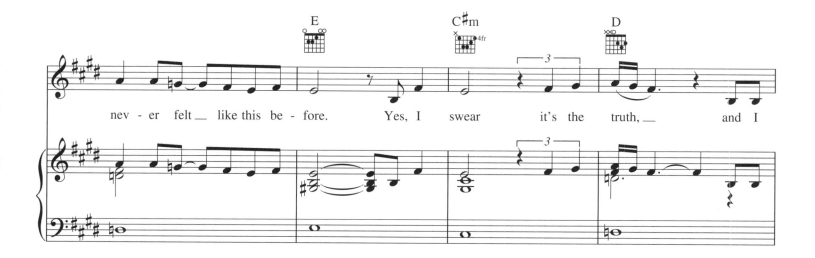

owe it all to you. _____

Male: I've been wait-ing for so long; _____ now I've

fi - n'lly found some-one _____ to stand by me.   *Female:* We saw the

writ - ing on the wall _____ as we felt this mag - i - cal _____ fan - ta -

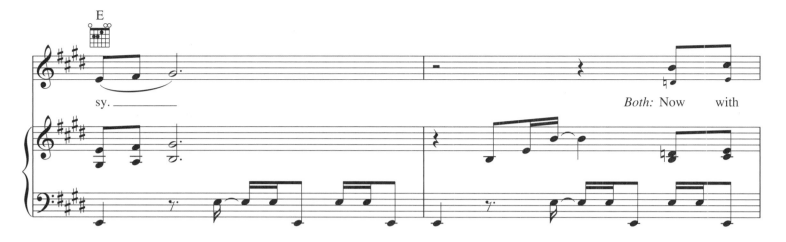

sy. _____   *Both:* Now   with

pas - sion in our eyes _____ there's   no   way   we   could _ dis - guise ____ it   se - cret -

ly. _____   So   we

take each oth - er's hand _____ 'cause we   seem   to un - der - stand _ the ur - gen -

cy.   *Male:* Just __ re - mem - ber,   *Female:* you're the

one thing   *Male:* I can't get e - nough __ of.   *Female:* So I'll tell you

some - thing: *Both:* this could be love.   Be - cause   I've __ had __

__ the time of my life. __   No, I nev - er felt __ this way be -

fore.   Yes, I   swear   it's the truth, _____   and I   owe it all to you. _____

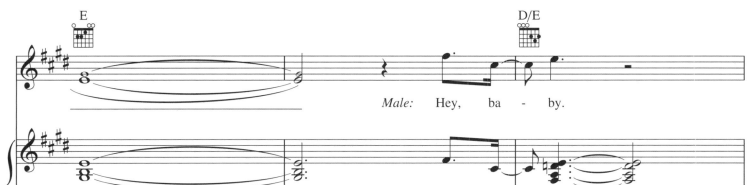

Male: Hey, ba - by.

Female: With   my   bod - y   and   soul, _____   I   want   you

more   than you'll ev   -   er   know. _   *Male:* So we'll

just let it go;___ don't be a-fraid to lose con-trol.___

Female: Yes, I know what's on ___ your mind when you say stay with me to-

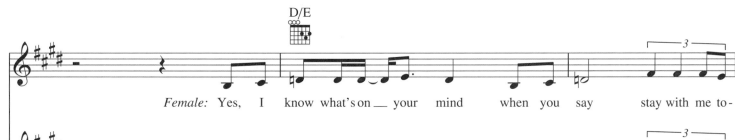

night._____ *Male:* Stay ___ with me. Just re-mem-ber, you're the

one thing ___ *Female:* I _____ can't get e-nough of. *Male:* So I'll tell you

some - thing: ___ *Both:* this could be love. Be - cause   I've ___ had ___

I've

___ the time of my   life. ___ No, I nev - er felt ___ this way be -

had the time of my   life. ___ And I've searched through ev -'ry o - pen

fore.   Yes, I swear it's the truth, _____ and I

door   till I've found the ___ truth, _____ and I

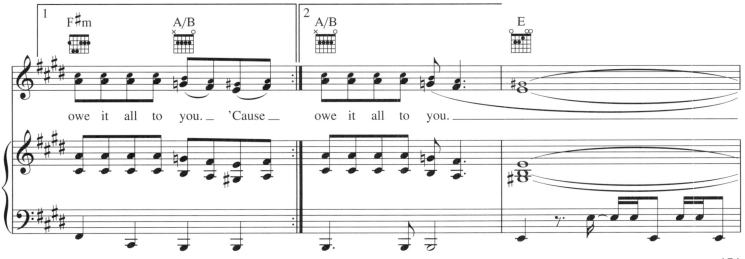

owe it all to you. ___ 'Cause ___ owe it all to you. _____

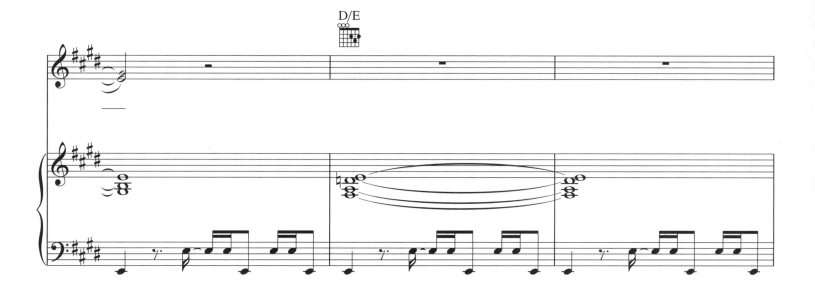

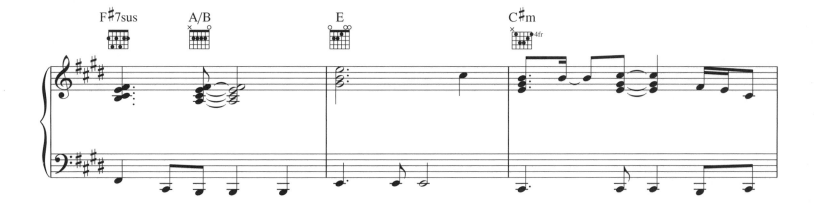

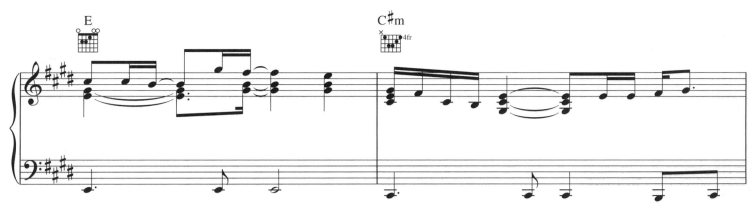

Male: Now

I've   had the time of my life. ___ No, I

Female: I've

mp

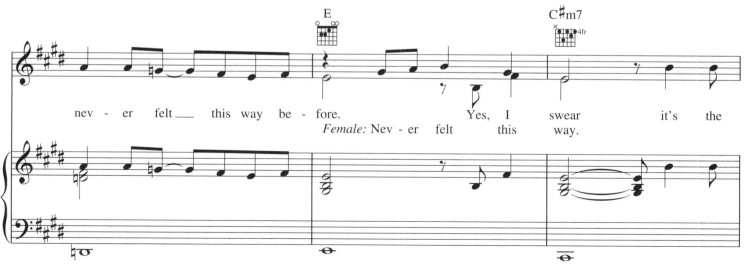

nev - er felt ___ this way be - fore.   Yes, I swear it's the

Female: Nev - er felt this way.

truth, ____ and I owe it all to you. ___ I've
I've

had the time of my life. ___ No, I nev - er felt __ this way be -
had the time of my life. ___ And I've searched through ev -'ry o - pen

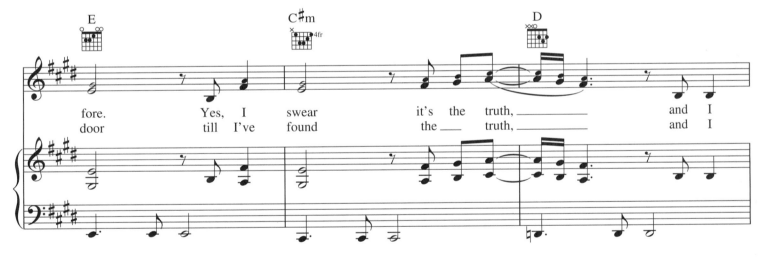

fore. Yes, I swear it's the truth, _____ and I
door till I've found the __ truth, _____ and I

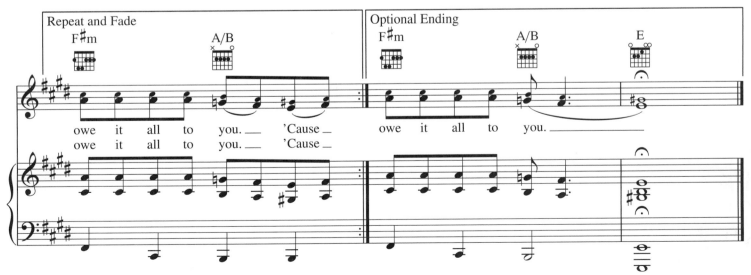

Repeat and Fade

owe it all to you. __ 'Cause __
owe it all to you. __ 'Cause __

Optional Ending

owe it all to you. _____

Isn't It Romantic?

from the Paramount Picture LOVE ME TONIGHT

Words by Lorenz Hart

Music by Richard Rodgers

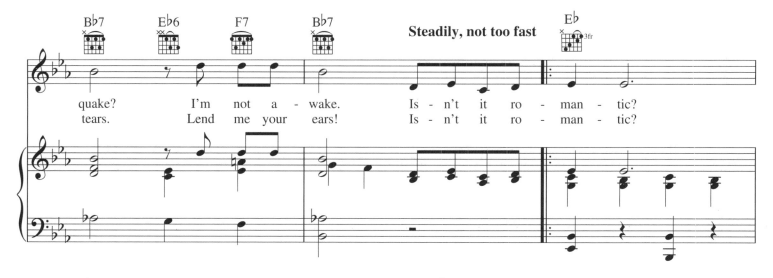

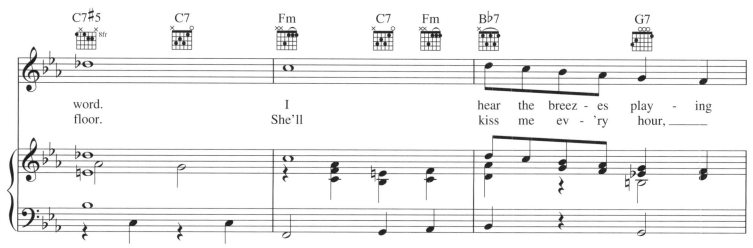

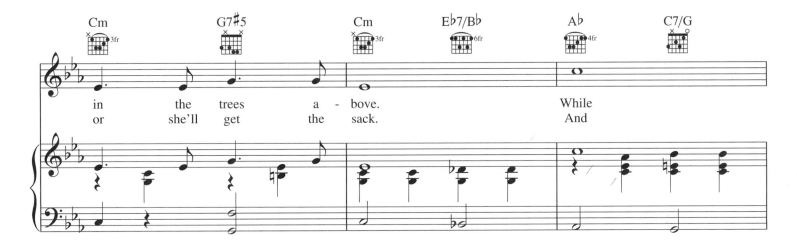

in the trees a - bove. While
or she'll get the sack. And

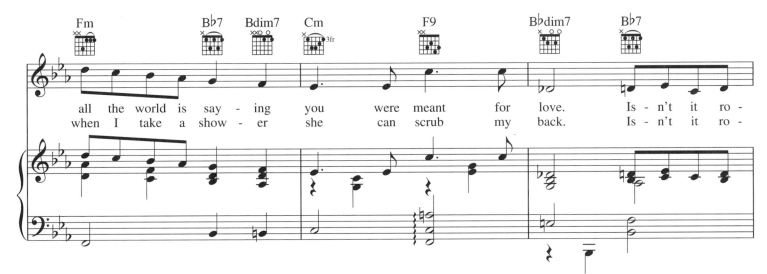

all the world is say - ing you were meant for love. Is - n't it ro -
when I take a show - er she can scrub my back. Is - n't it ro -

man - tic? Mere - ly to be young on such a night as
man - tic? On a moon - light night she'll cook me on - ion

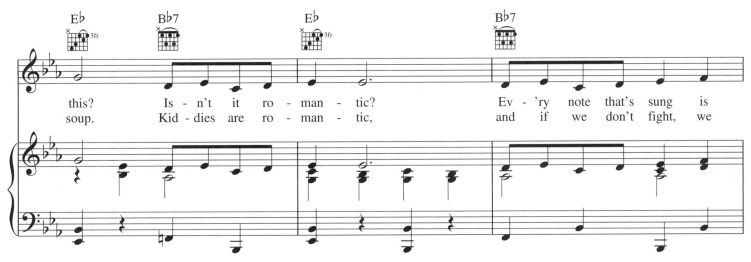

this? Is - n't it ro - man - tic? Ev - 'ry note that's sung is
soup. Kid - dies are ro - man - tic, and if we don't fight, we

like a lov - er's kiss. Sweet
soon will have a troupe! We'll

sym - bols in the moon - light, do you mean that I will fall in
help the pop - u - la - tion, it's a du - ty that we owe in to

love per - chance? _____ Is - n't it ro - mance?
dear old France. _____ Is - n't it ro -

Is - n't it ro - mance? _____

It's Only a Paper Moon

featured in the Motion Picture TAKE A CHANCE

Lyric by
Billy Rose and E.Y. "Yip" Harburg

Music by Harold Arlen

Say, it's on-ly a pa-per moon, ___ sail-ing o-ver a card-board sea, ___

but it would-n't be make be-lieve, ___ if you ___ be-lieved ___ in me. ___

Yes, it's on-ly a can-vas sky, _ hang-ing o-ver a mus-lin tree, _

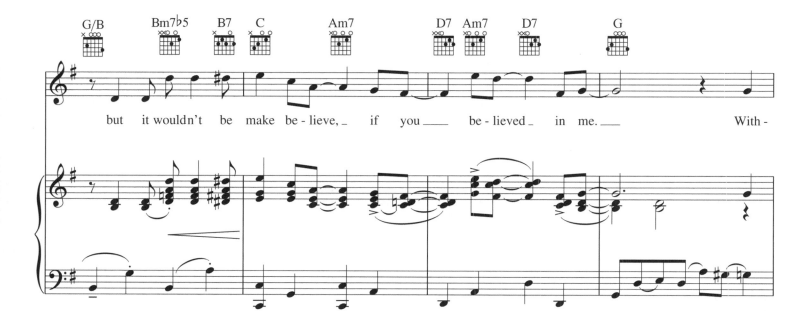

but it wouldn't be make be-lieve, _ if you ____ be-lieved _ in me. _ With-

out your love, it's a hon-ky-tonk pa-rade. With-out your

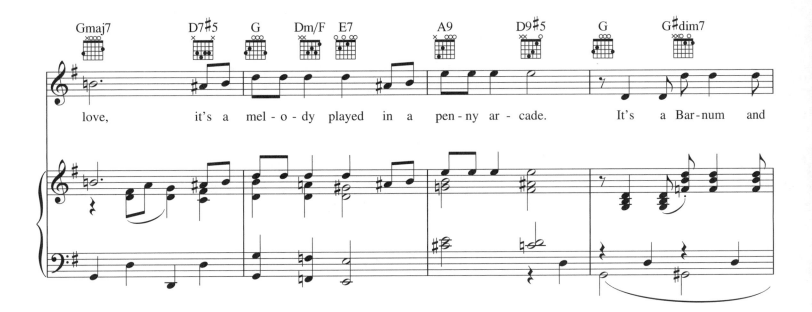

love, it's a mel - o - dy played in a pen - ny ar - cade. It's a Bar - num and

Bai - ley world, __ just as pho - ny as it can be, __ But it would - n't be

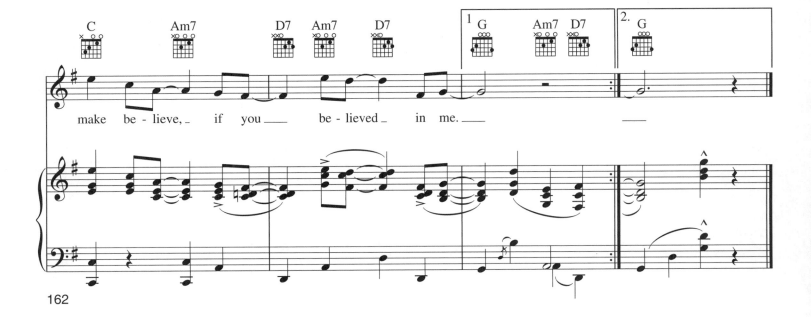

make be - lieve, __ if you __ be - lieved __ in me. __

James Bond Theme

from DR. NO

By Monty Norman

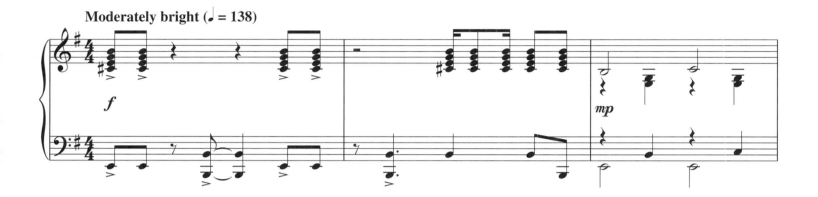

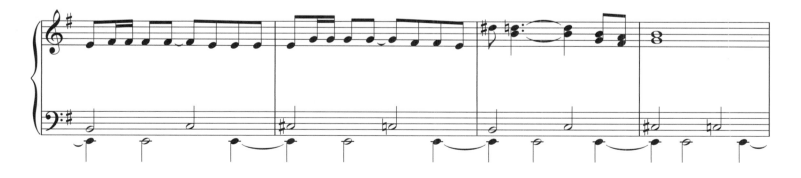

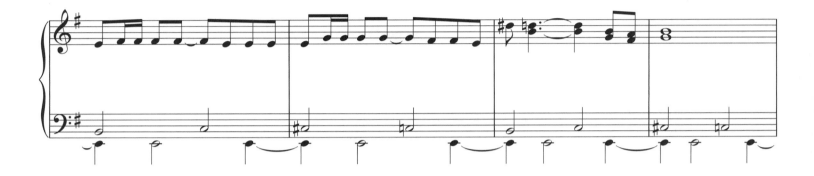

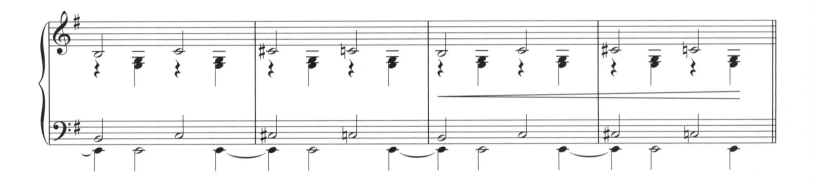

With a slight Swing feel

Tempo I

The John Dunbar Theme

from DANCES WITH WOLVES

By John Barry

Moderately

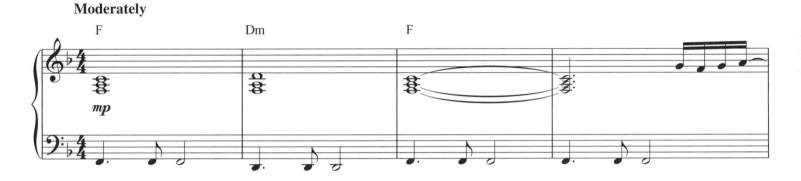

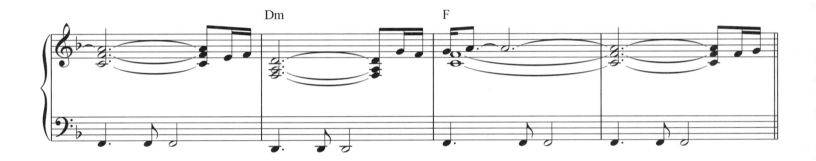

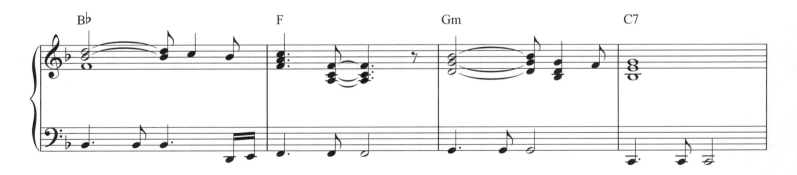

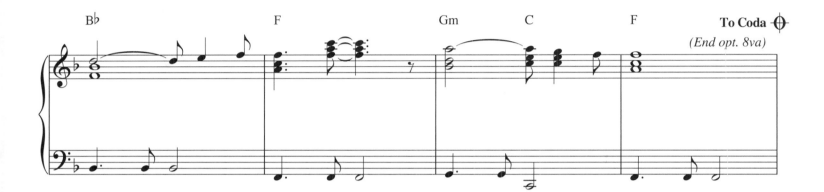

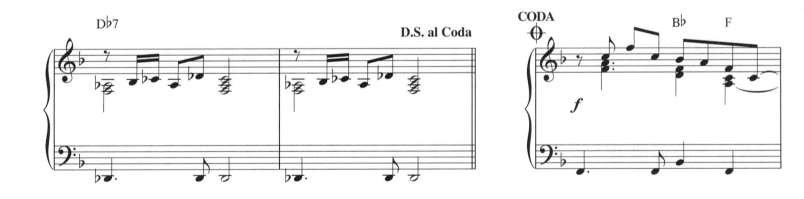

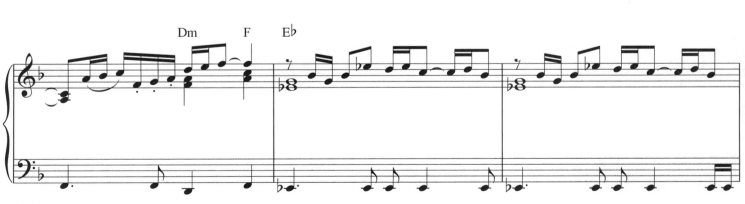

168

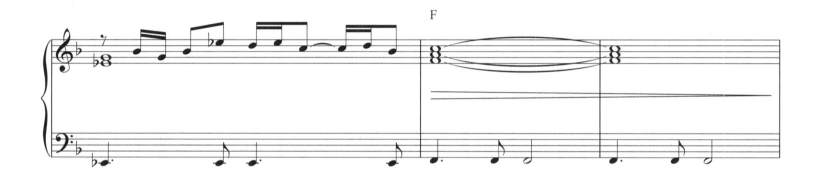

169

Let the River Run

Theme from the Motion Picture WORKING GIRL

Words and Music by
Carly Simon

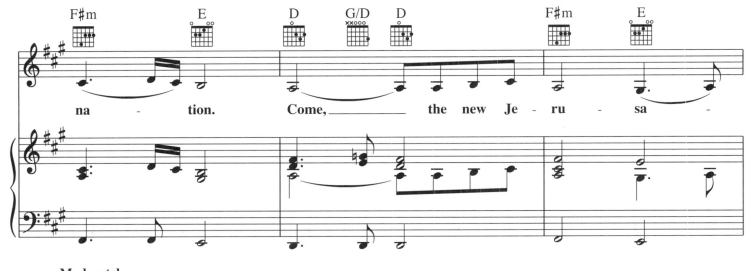

na - tion. Come, _____ the new Je - ru - sa -

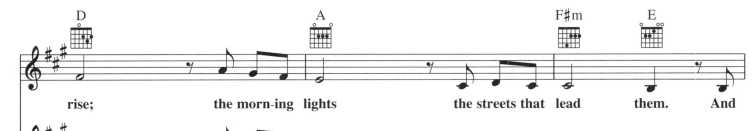

lem. Sil - ver cit-ies

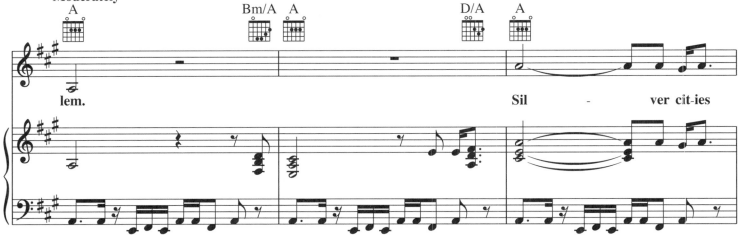

rise; the morn-ing lights the streets that lead them. And

si - rens call them on with a song.

It's ask - ing for the tak - ing,

trem - bling, sha - ak - ing.__ Oh, _____ my heart is

ach - ing. We're com-ing to the edge, run - ning on the wa - ter,

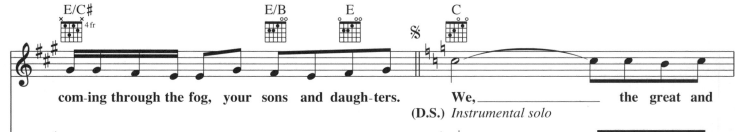

com-ing through the fog, your sons and daugh-ters. We,_____ the great and

(D.S.) *Instrumental solo*

172

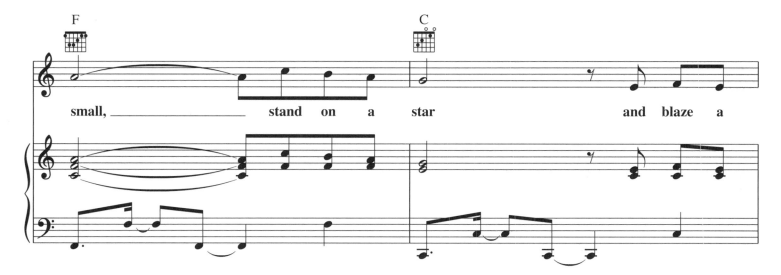

small, _____ stand on a star and blaze a

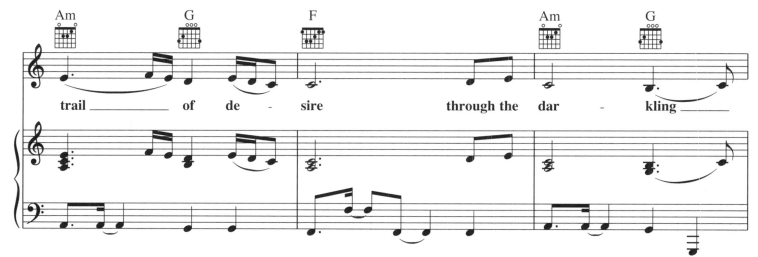

trail _____ of de - sire through the dar - kling _____

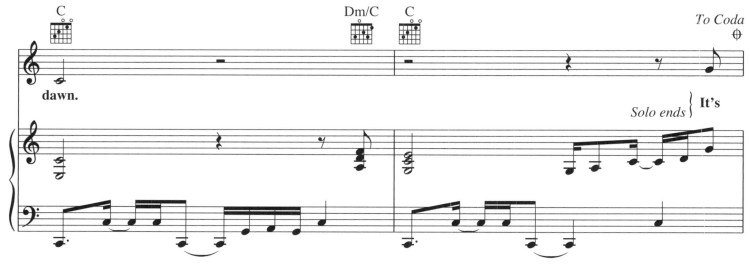

To Coda ⊕

dawn. *Solo ends* It's

ask - ing for the tak - ing. Come run with me now; the sky is the col-or of

173

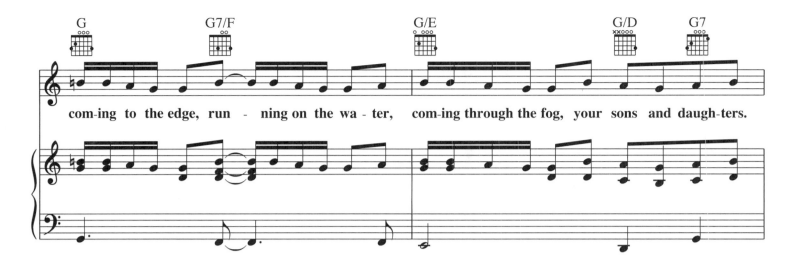

com-ing to the edge, run - ning on the wa - ter, com-ing through the fog, your sons and daugh-ters.

Let _____ the riv-er run, _____ let all the dream - ers wake the

na - tion. Come, _____ the new Je - ru - sa -

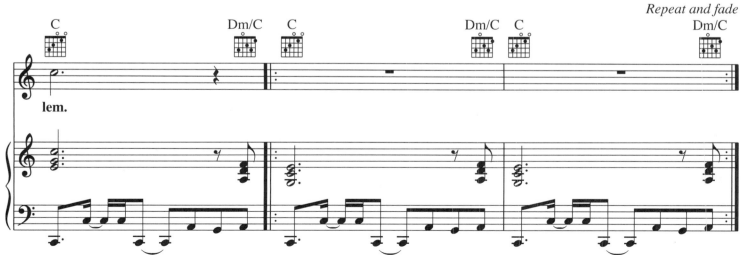

lem.

The Man That Got Away

from the Motion Picture A STAR IS BORN

Lyric by Ira Gershwin

Music by Harold Arlen

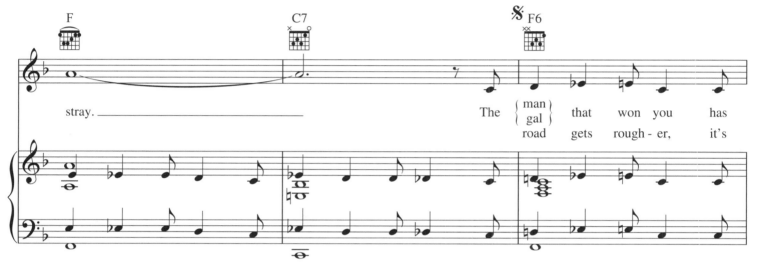

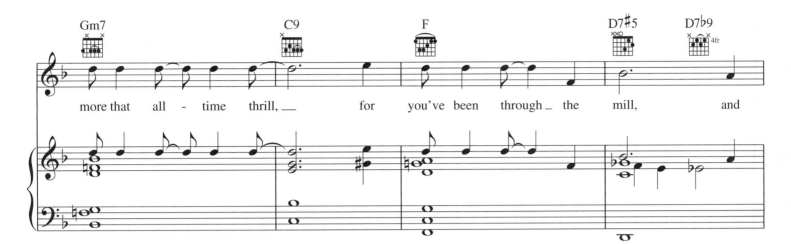

more that all - time thrill, __ for you've been through __ the mill, and

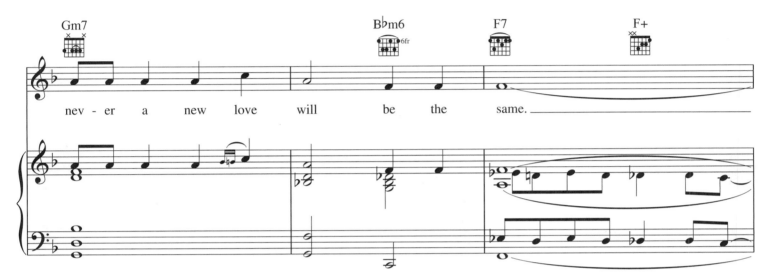

nev - er a new love will be the same. __

__ Good rid - dance! Good - bye! Ev -'ry trick of {his}{hers} you're on

to; but, fools __ will be fools, and where's {he}{she} gone to? __ The

D.S. al Coda

CODA

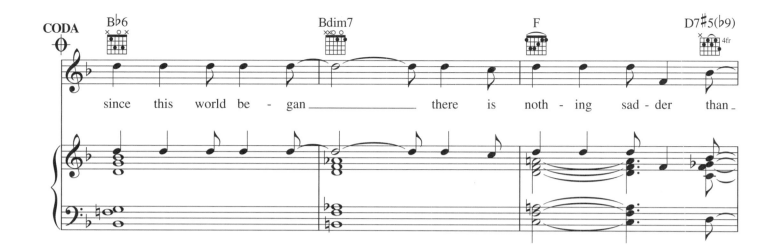

since this world be - gan _____ there is noth - ing sad - der than ___

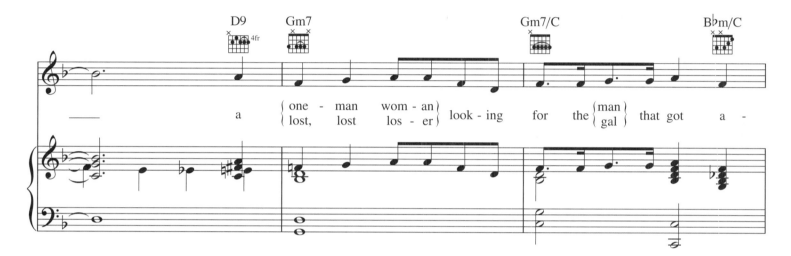

___ a {one - man wom - an / lost, lost los - er} look - ing for the {man / gal} that got a -

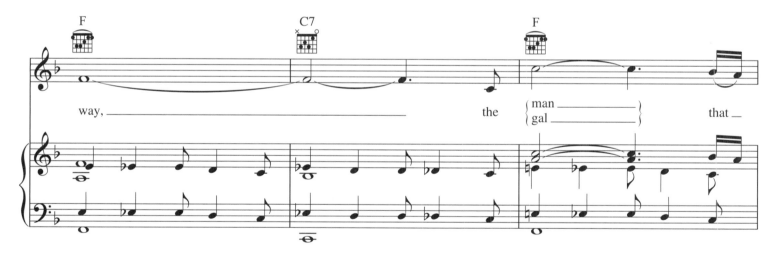

way, _____ the {man _____ / gal _____} that ___

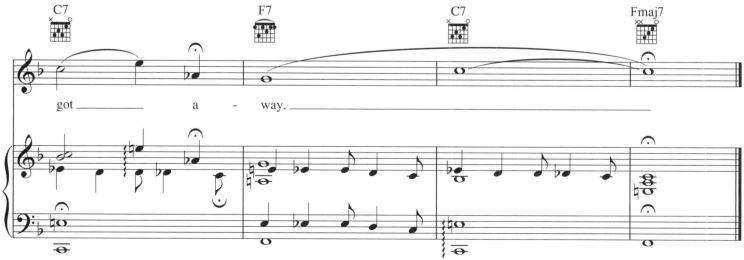

got _____ a - way. _____

Midnight Cowboy

from the Motion Picture MIDNIGHT COWBOY

Lyric by Jack Gold

Music by John Barry

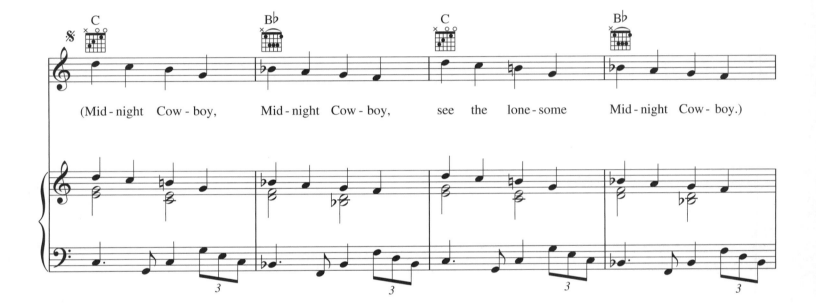

(Mid-night Cow-boy, Mid-night Cow-boy, see the lone-some Mid-night Cow-boy.)

Once ___ his hopes were high ___ as the sky, once ___ a dream was

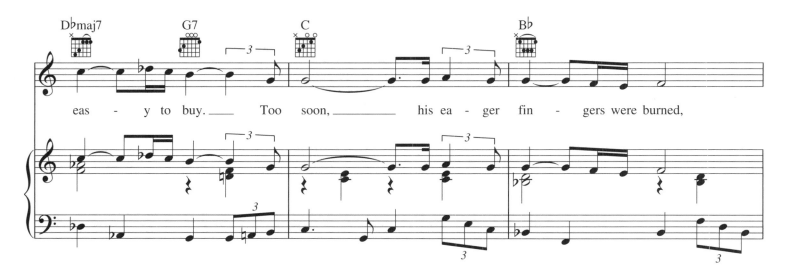

eas - - y to buy. _____ Too soon, _____ his ea - ger fin - gers were burned,

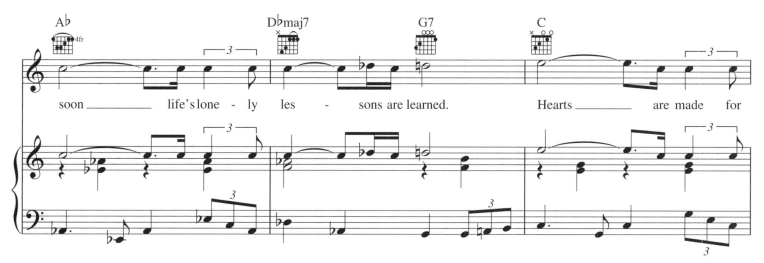

soon _____ life's lone - ly les - sons are learned. Hearts _____ are made for

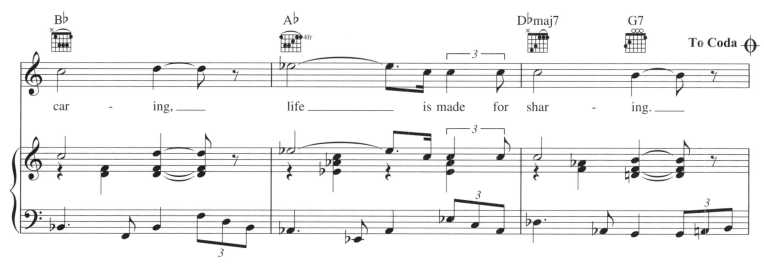

car - - ing, _____ life _____ is made for shar - ing. _____

Love _____ is all that's left _____ in the end.

D.S. al Coda

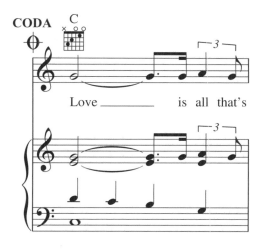

CODA

Love _____ is all that's

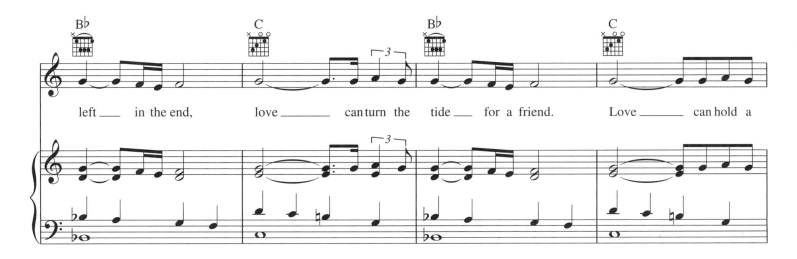

left ____ in the end, love _____ can turn the tide ____ for a friend. Love _____ can hold a

dream to - geth - er, love _____ is all that lasts for - ev - er. Love _____ is all that's

left _____ in the end, love _____ can turn the tide ____ for a friend.

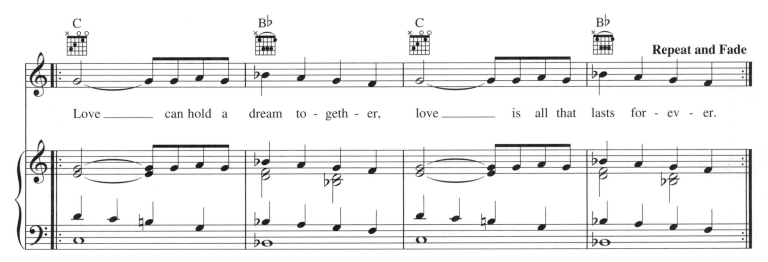

Love _____ can hold a dream to - geth - er, love _____ is all that lasts for - ev - er.

Mrs. Robinson

from THE GRADUATE

Words and Music by
Paul Simon

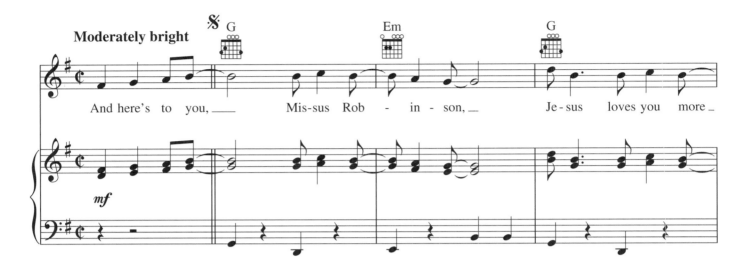

And here's to you, ___ Mis-sus Rob - in - son, ___ Je-sus loves you more ___

___ than you ___ will know. _____ (Wo, wo, wo.) ___

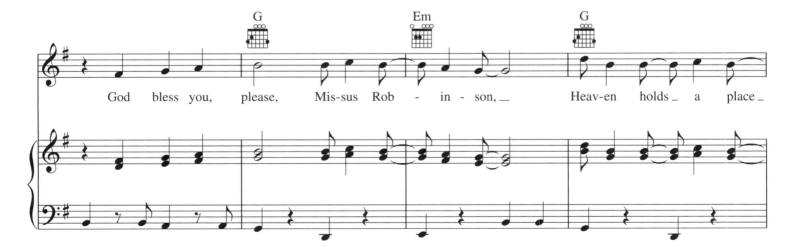

God bless you, please, Mis-sus Rob - in - son, ___ Heav-en holds ___ a place ___

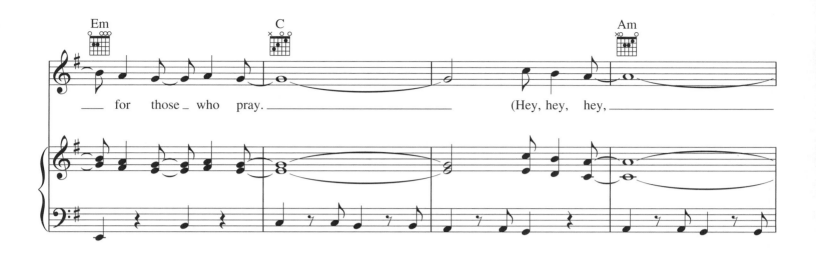

for those _ who pray. _____ (Hey, hey, hey, _____

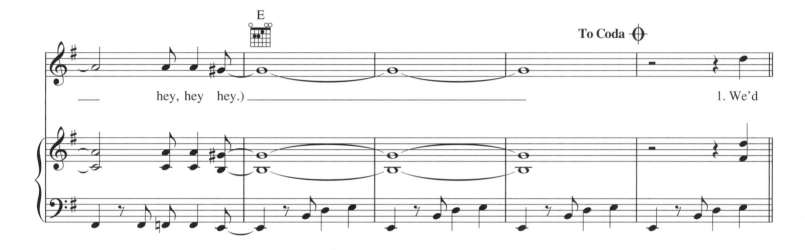

_ hey, hey hey.) _____

To Coda ⊕

1. We'd

like to know a lit - tle bit _ a - bout _ you for our files, _____

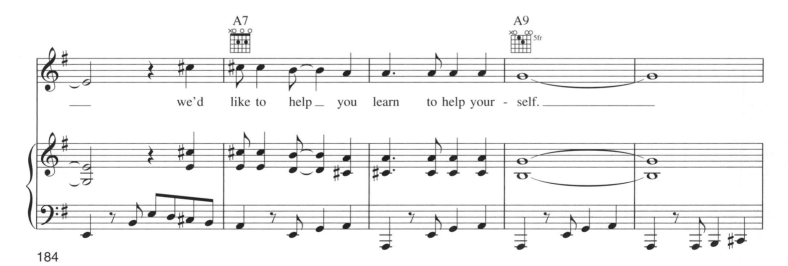

_ we'd like to help _ you learn to help your - self. _____

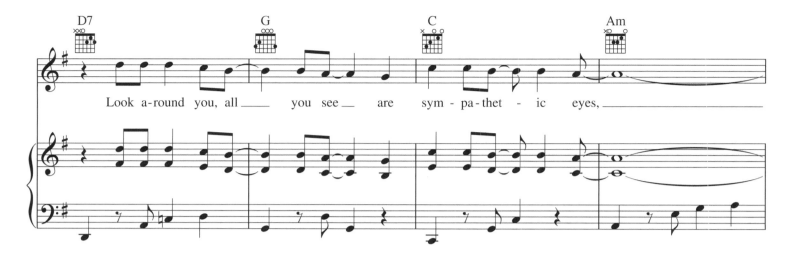

Look a-round you, all ___ you see ___ are sym-pa-thet-ic eyes, ___

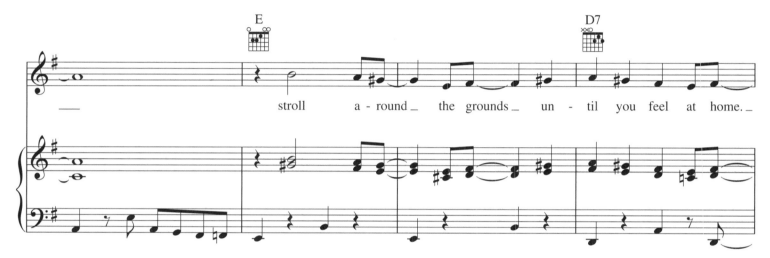

stroll a-round ___ the grounds ___ un-til you feel at home. ___

D.S. al Coda

___ And here's to you, _

CODA

E7

2. Hide it in a hid — ing place ___ where
3. Sit-ting on a so - fa on ___ a

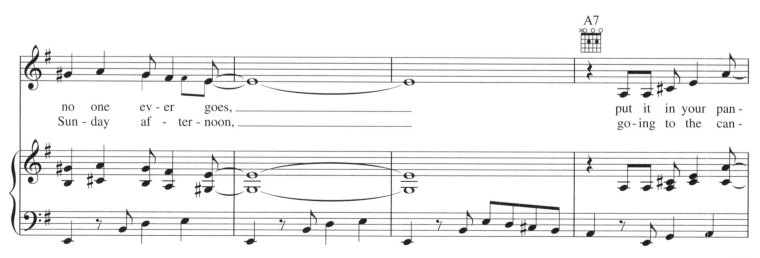

A7

no one ev - er goes, _____
Sun - day af - ter-noon, _____

put it in your pan-
go-ing to the can-

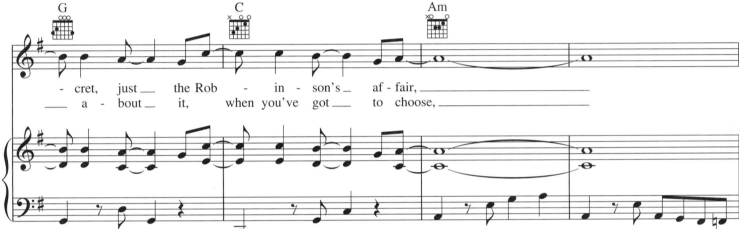

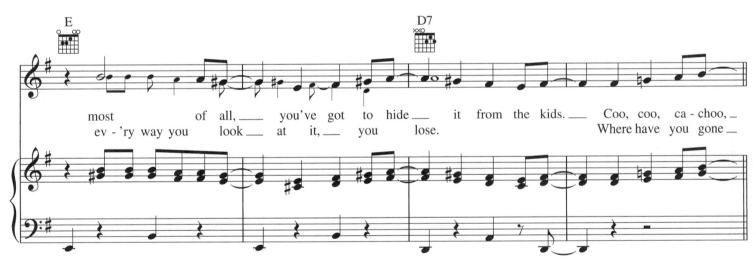

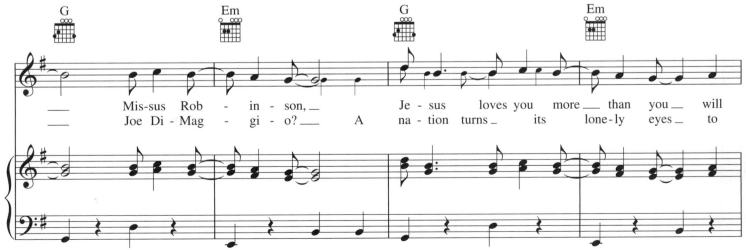

know. _____ (Wo, wo, wo.) _ God bless you
you. _____ (Woo, woo, woo.) _ What's that you

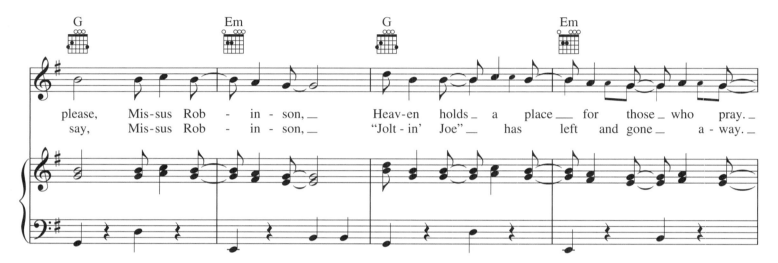

please, Mis-sus Rob - in - son, _ Heav-en holds _ a place _ for those _ who pray. _
say, Mis-sus Rob - in - son, _ "Jolt-in' Joe" _ has left and gone _ a - way. _

(Hey, hey, hey, _____ hey, hey, hey.) _
(Hey, hey, hey, _____ hey, hey, hey.) _

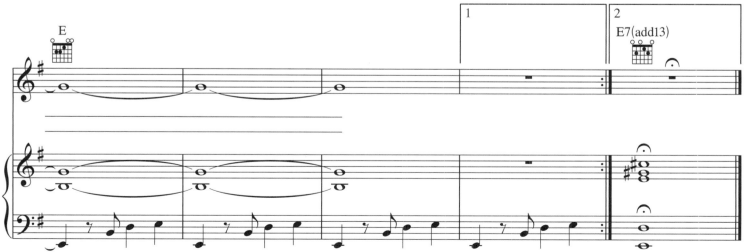

Moon River

from the Paramount Picture BREAKFAST AT TIFFANY'S

Words by Johnny Mercer

Music by Henry Mancini

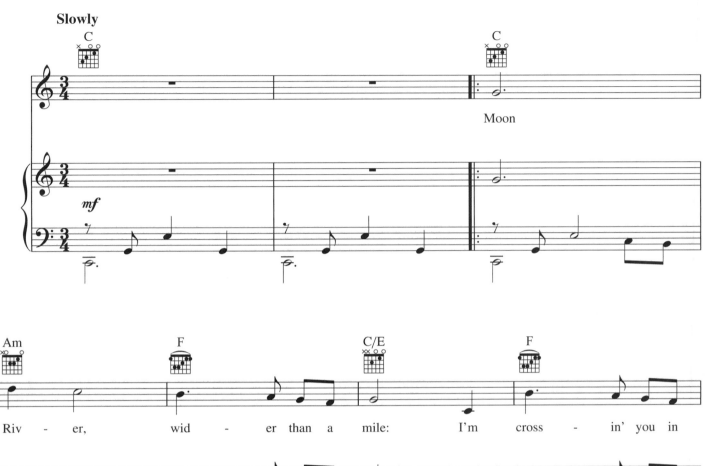

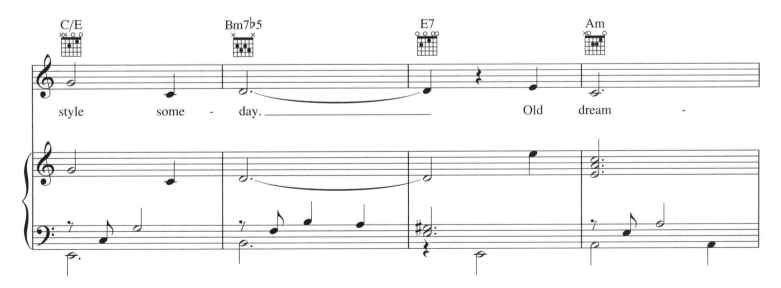

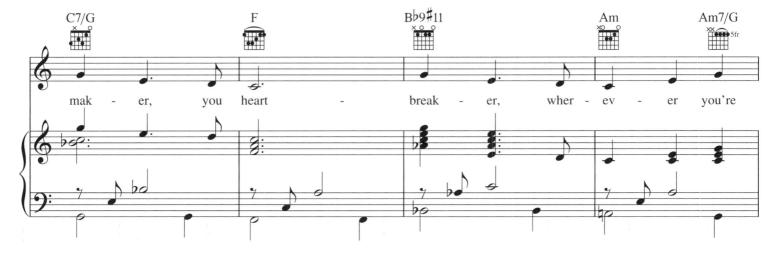

maker, you heart - break - er, wher - ev - er you're

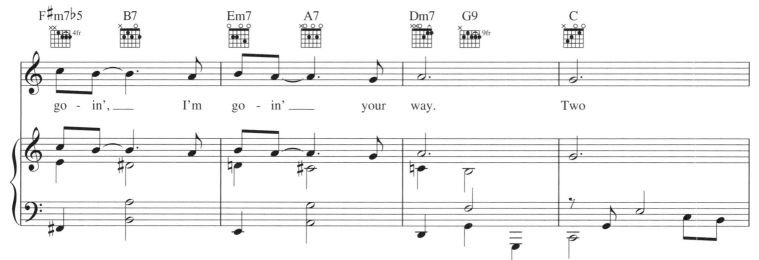

go - in', ___ I'm go - in' ___ your way. Two

drift - ers, off to see the world. There's such a lot of

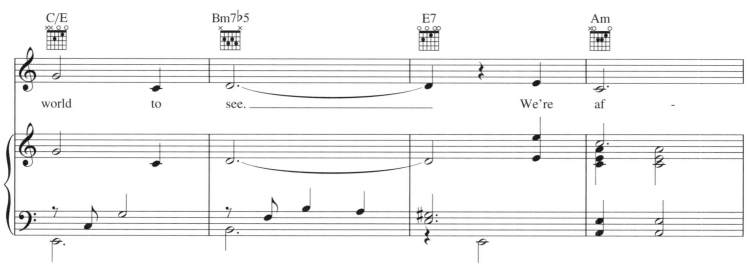

world to see. _____ We're af -

Moonlight Becomes You

from the Paramount Picture ROAD TO MOROCCO

Words by Johnny Burke

Music by James Van Heusen

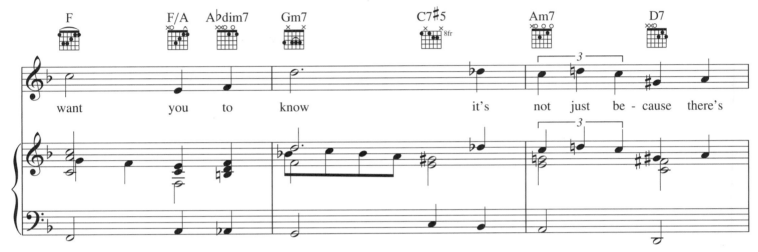

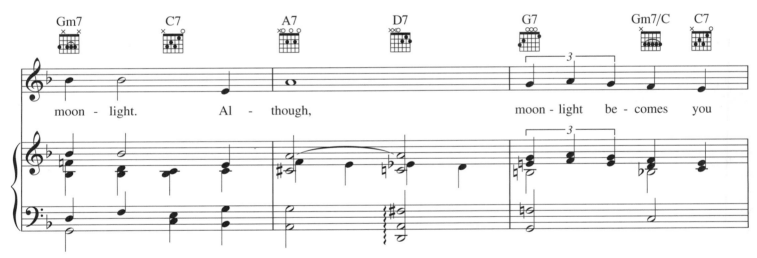

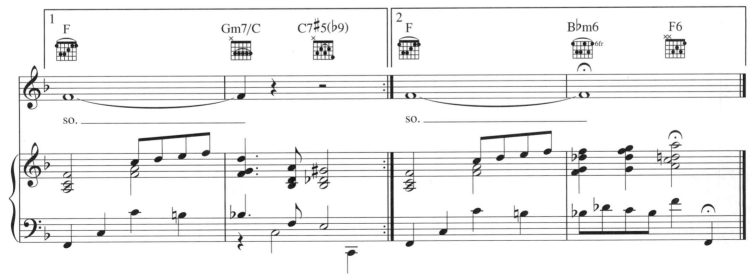

More

(Ti guarderò nel cuore)

from the Film MONDO CANE

Italian Lyrics by Marcello Ciorciolini
English Lyrics by Norman Newell

Music by
Nino Oliviero and Riz Ortolani

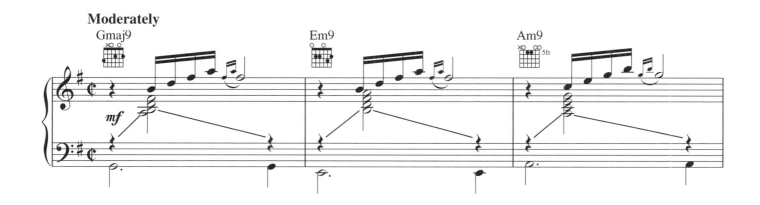

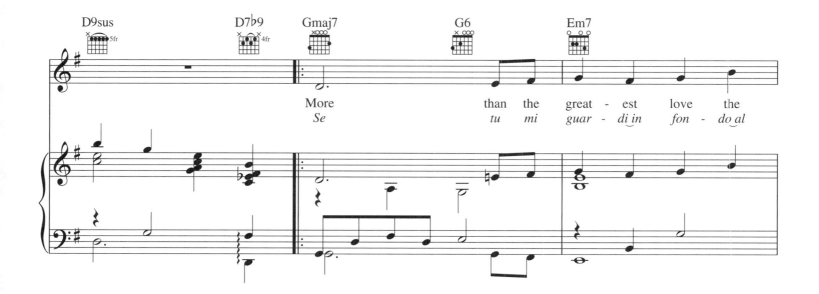

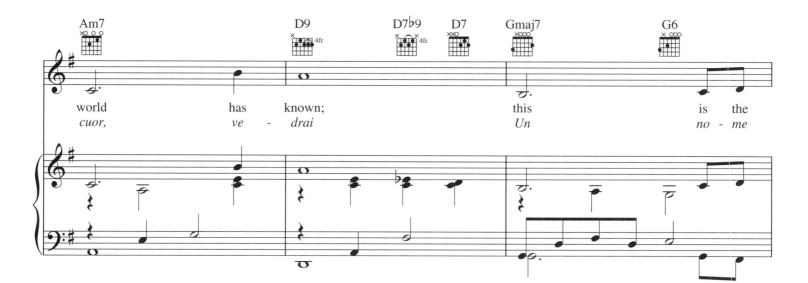

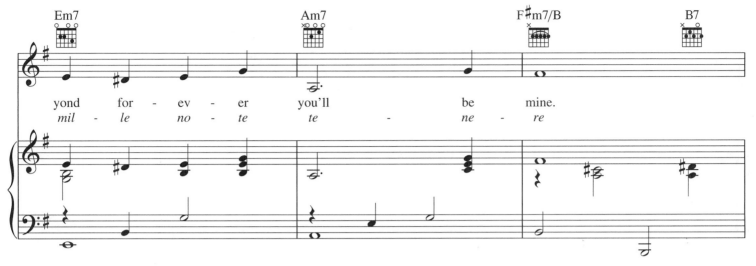

yond for - ev - er you'll be mine.
mil - le no - te te - ne - re

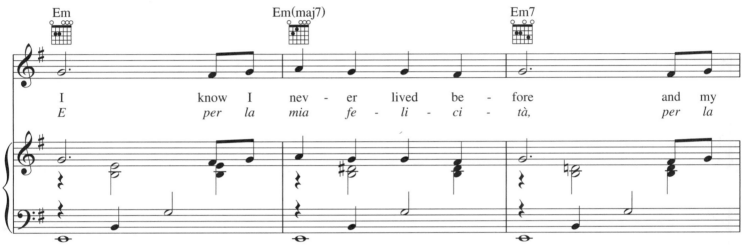

I know I nev - er lived be - fore and my
E per la mia fe - li - ci - tà, per la

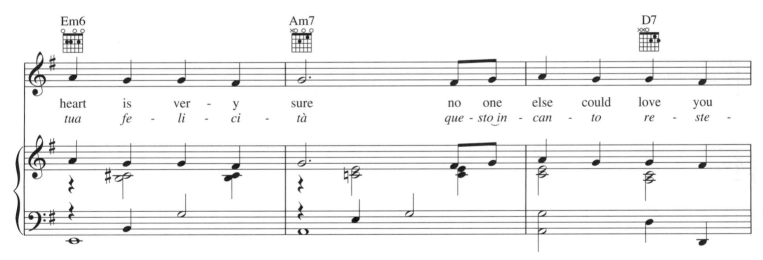

heart is ver - y sure no one else could love you
tua fe - li - ci - tà que - sto in - can - to re - ste -

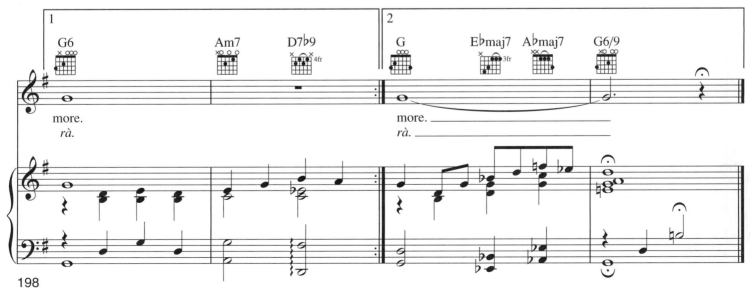

more.
rà.

more.
rà.

My Heart Will Go On

(Love Theme from 'Titanic')

from the Paramount and Twentieth Century Fox Motion Picture TITANIC

Lyric by Will Jennings

Music by James Horner

Ev - 'ry night in my dreams I see you, I

feel you, that is how I know you go on.

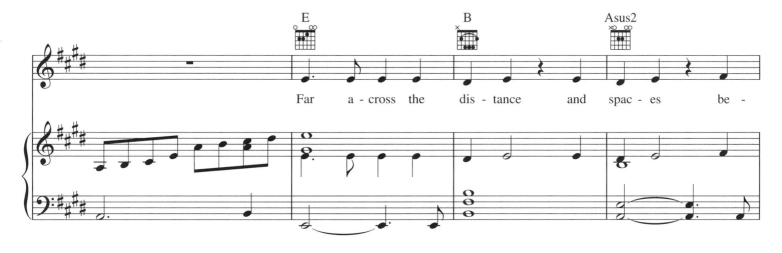

Far a-cross the dis-tance and spac-es be-

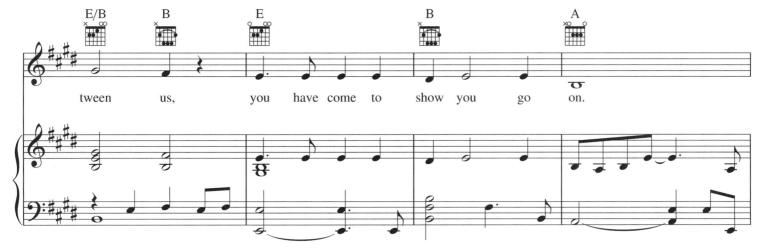

tween us, you have come to show you go on.

Near, far, wher-ev-er you are,

I be-lieve that the heart does go on.

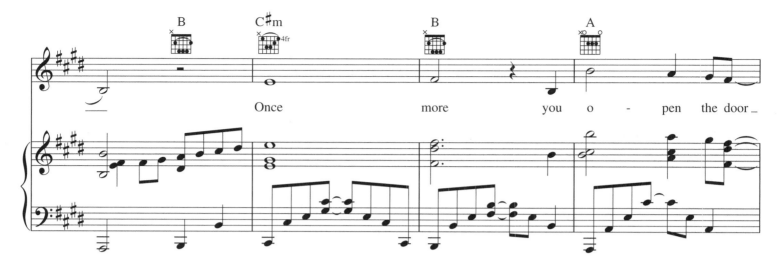

Once more you o - pen the door _

_ and you're here in my heart, and my heart will go

To Coda ⊕

on and on.

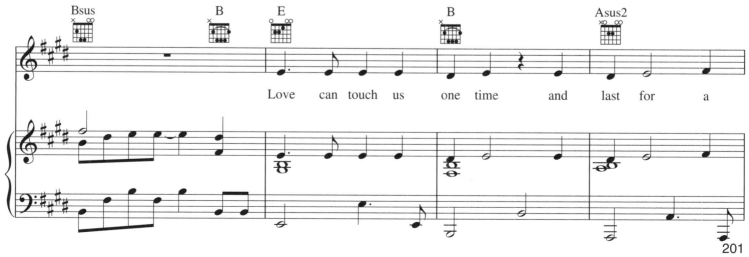

Love can touch us one time and last for a

life - time, and nev - er let go till we're gone.

Love was when I loved you; one true time I

hold to. In my life we'll al - ways go on.

D.S. al Coda

CODA

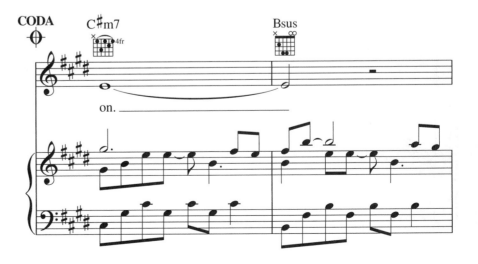

on.

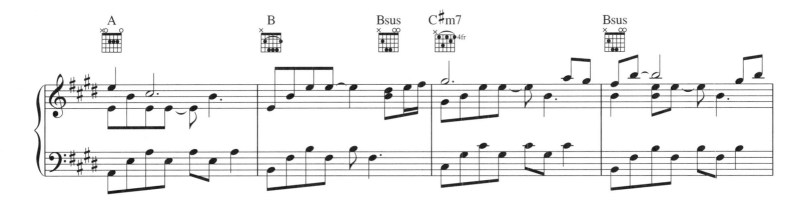

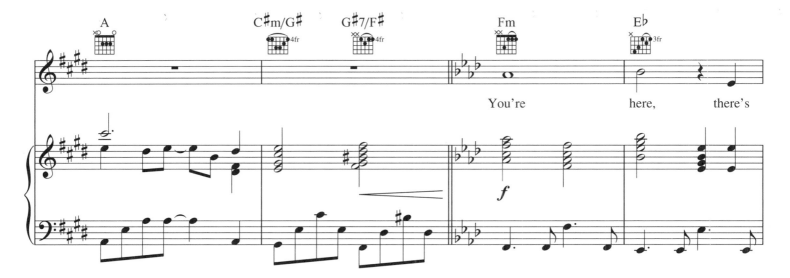

You're here, there's

noth - ing I fear ___ and I know ___ that my heart will go

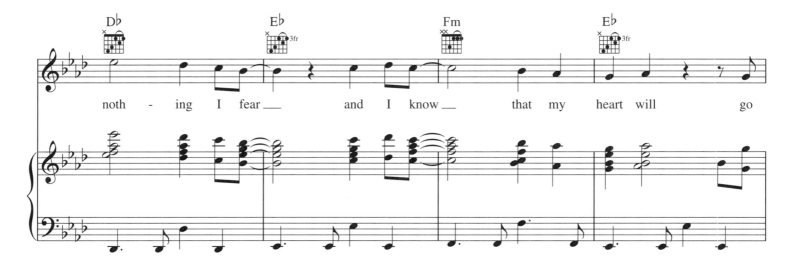

on. ___ We'll stay for -

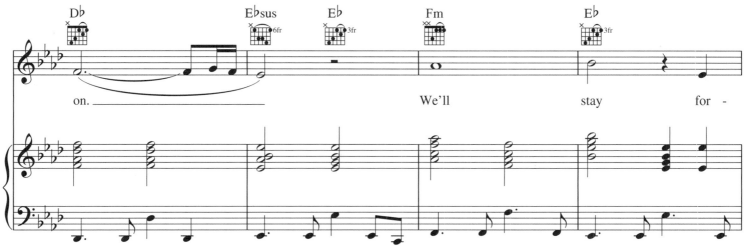

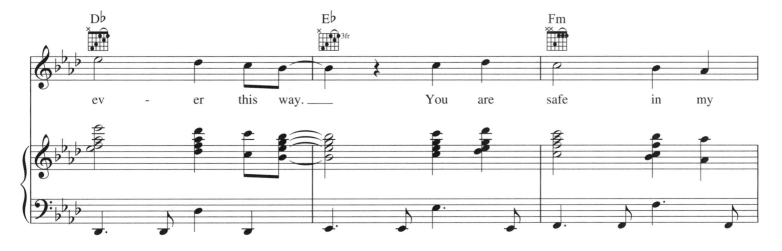

ev - er this way. ____ You are safe in my

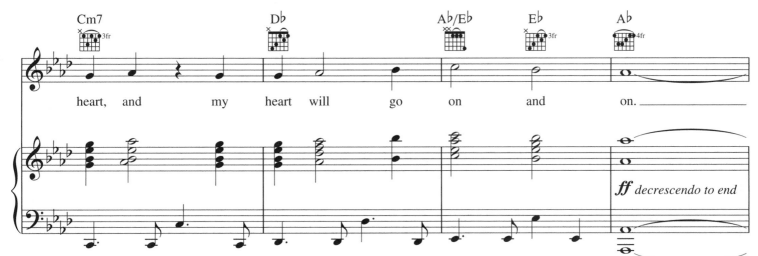

heart, and my heart will go on and on. ____

ff *decrescendo to end*

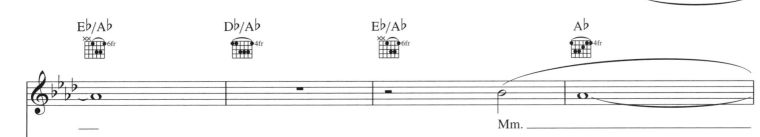

Mm. ____

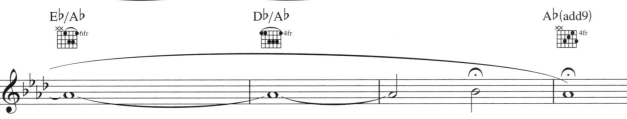

Theme from "New York, New York"

from NEW YORK, NEW YORK

Words by Fred Ebb

Music by John Kander

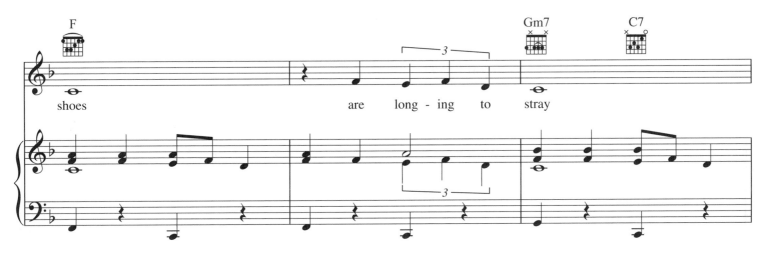

shoes   are long - ing to stray

and step a - round the heart __ of it,   New York, New
(D.S.) *Instrumental*

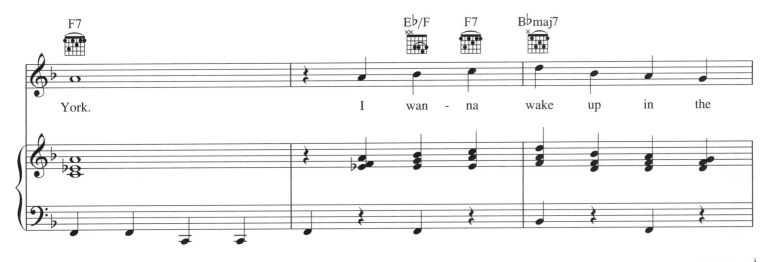

York.   I wan - na wake up in the

To Coda

cit - y that does - n't sleep   to find I'm

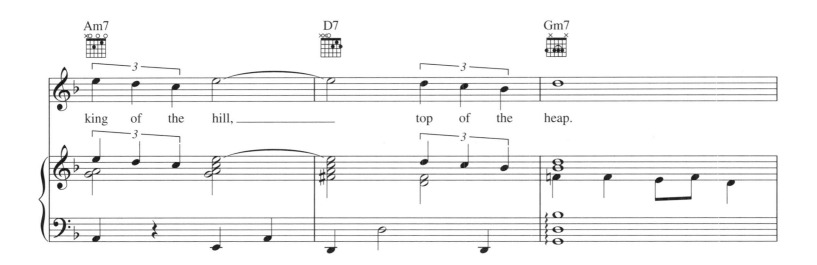

king of the hill, _____ top of the heap.

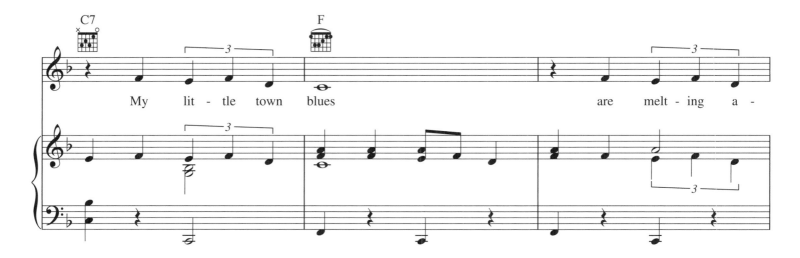

My lit - tle town blues are melt - ing a -

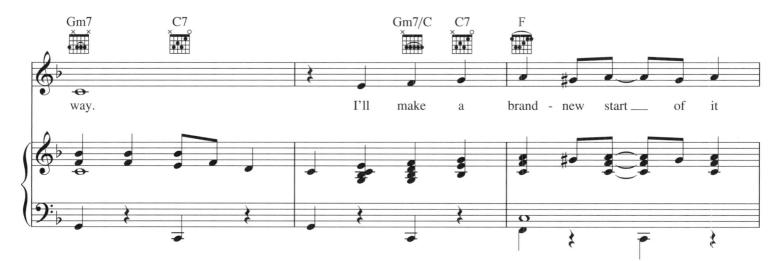

way. I'll make a brand - new start __ of it

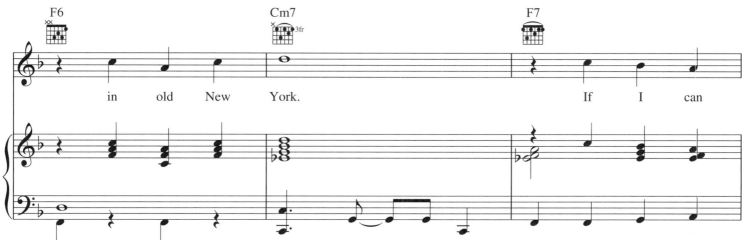

in old New York. If I can

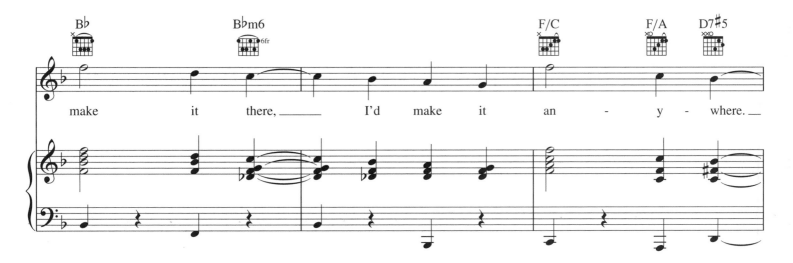

make it there, ____ I'd make it an - y - where. ____

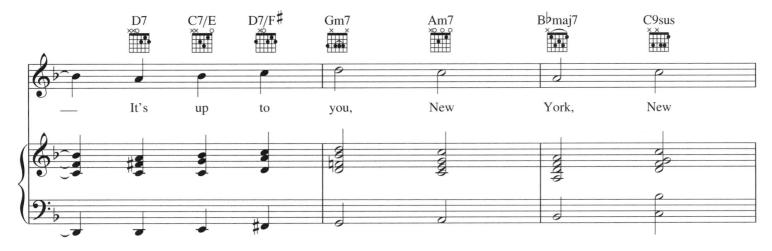

____ It's up to you, New York, New

York.

D.S. al Coda

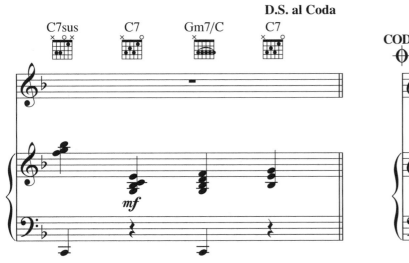

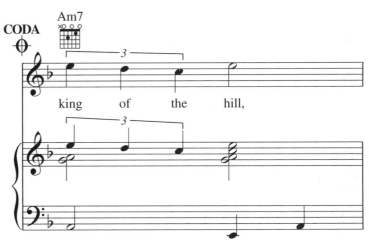

CODA

king of the hill,

head of the list, cream of the crop at the top of the heap. My lit-tle town blues are melt-ing a-way. I'll make a

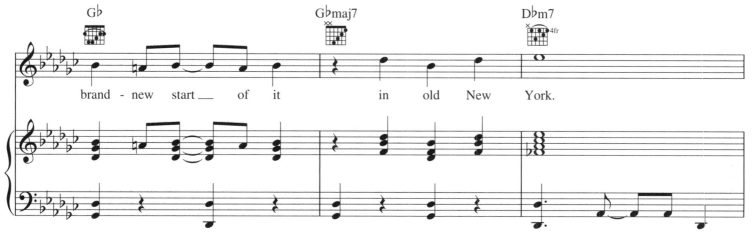

brand - new start __ of it in old New York.

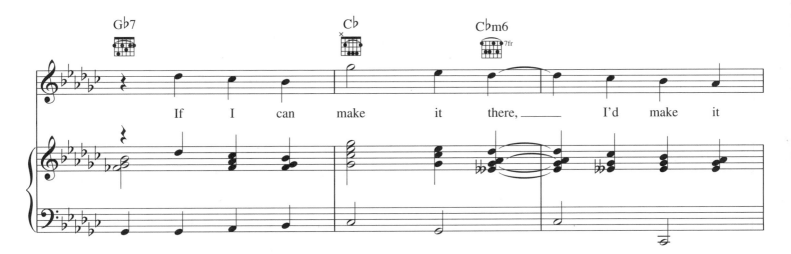

If I can make it there, _____ I'd make it

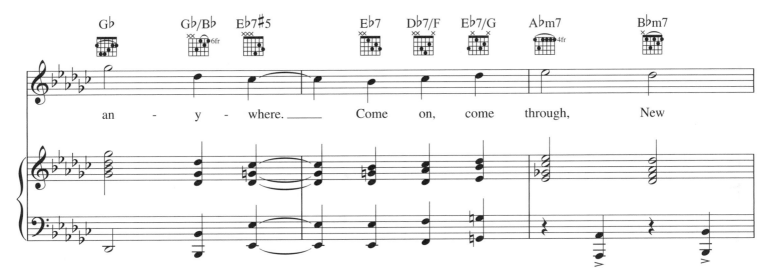

an - y - where. _____ Come on, come through, New

York, New York. _____

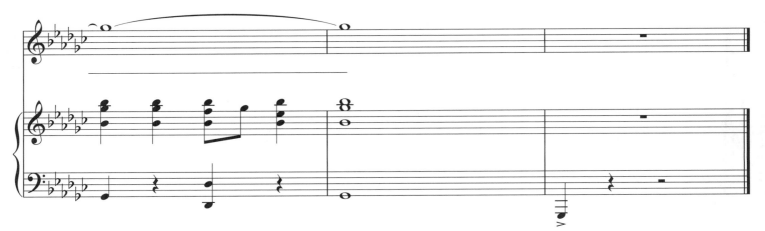

Nobody Does It Better

from THE SPY WHO LOVED ME

Lyrics by Carole Bayer Sager

Music by Marvin Hamlisch

One for My Baby

(And One More for the Road)

from the Motion Picture THE SKY'S THE LIMIT

Lyric by Johnny Mercer

Music by Harold Arlen

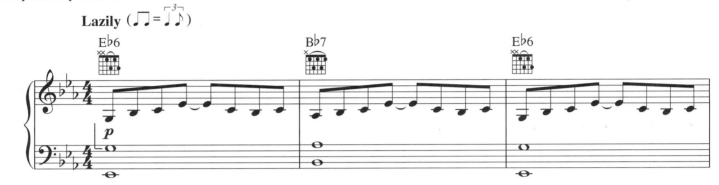

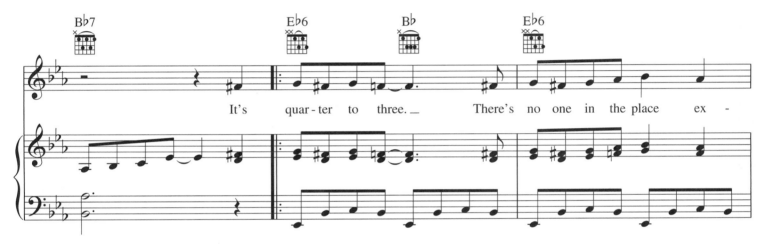

It's quar-ter to three. _ There's no one in the place ex-

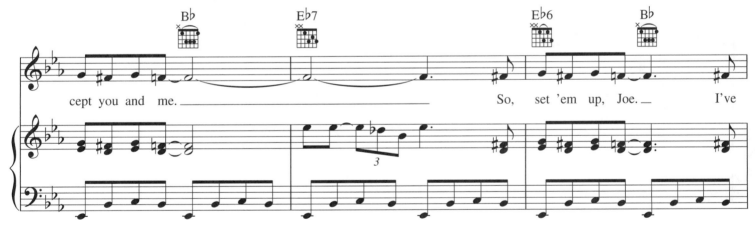

cept you and me. _____ So, set 'em up, Joe. _ I've

got a lit-tle sto-ry you ought-a know. _____ We're

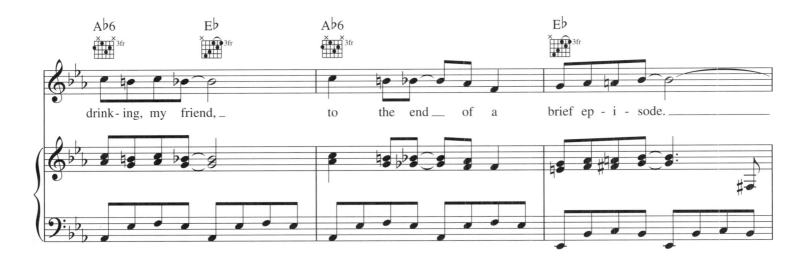

drink-ing, my friend, __ to the end __ of a brief ep-i-sode. __

__ Make it one for my ba-by and one more for the road.

I got the rou-tine, __ so drop an-oth-er nick-el

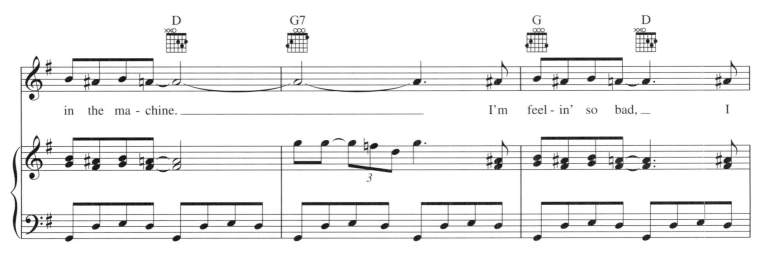

in the ma-chine. __ I'm feel-in' so bad, __ I

wish you'd make the mu - sic dream-y and sad. _____ Could

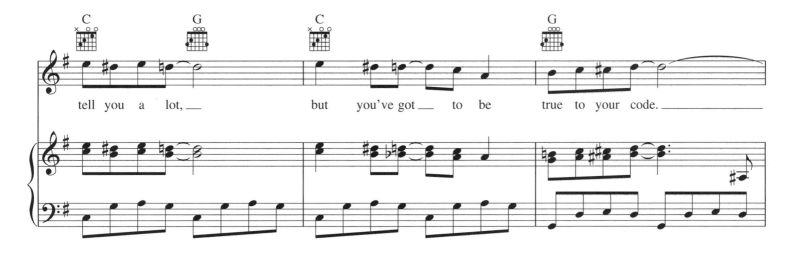

tell you a lot, ___ but you've got ___ to be true to your code. _____

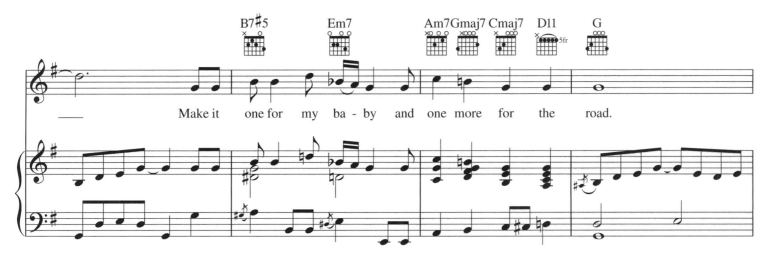

___ Make it one for my ba - by and one more for the road.

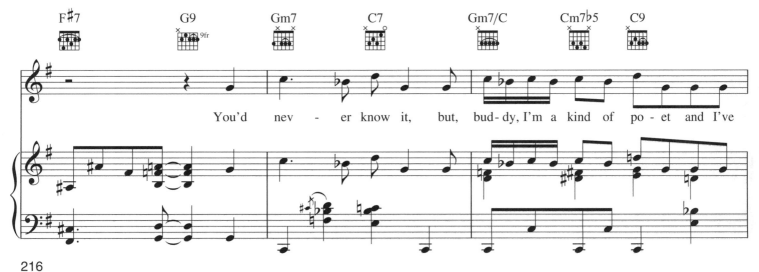

You'd nev - er know it, but, bud-dy, I'm a kind of po - et and I've

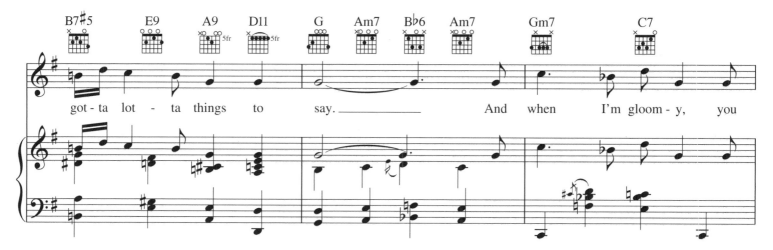

got-ta lot-ta things to say. _____ And when I'm gloom-y, you

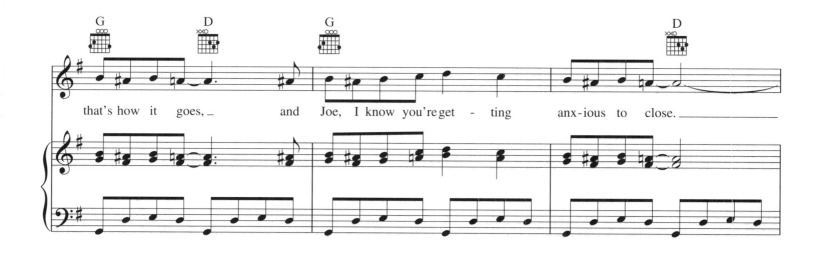

sim-ply got-ta lis-ten to me un-til it's talked a-way. _____ Well,

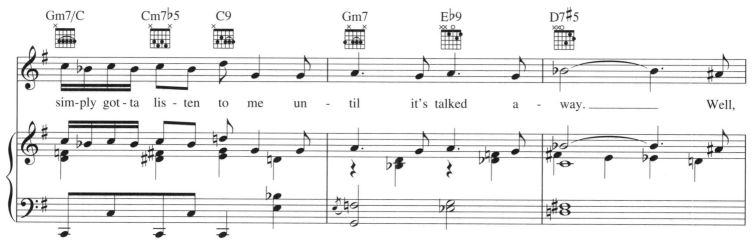

that's how it goes, _ and Joe, I know you're get-ting anx-ious to close. _____

_____ So, thanks for the cheer. _ I hope you did-n't mind my

bend-ing your ear. _____ This torch that I've found _

must be drowned _ or it soon might ex-plode. _____ Make it one for my ba-by and

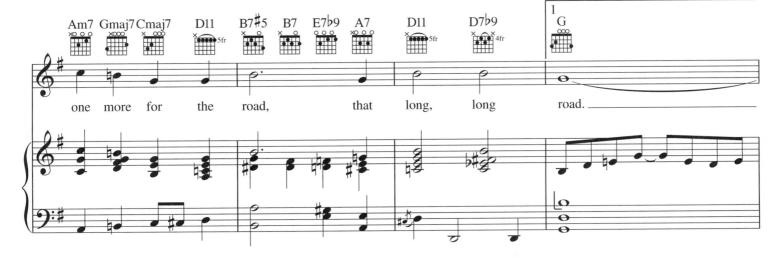

one more for the road, that long, long road. _____

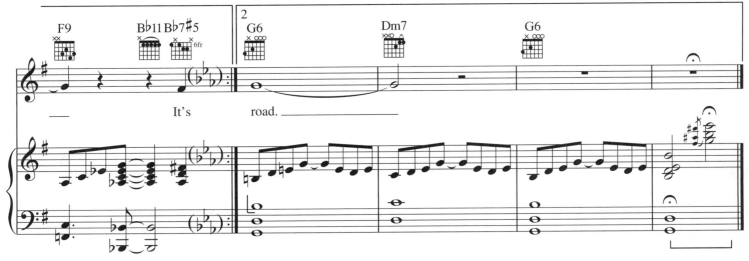

It's road.

Over the Rainbow

from THE WIZARD OF OZ

Lyric by E.Y. "Yip" Harburg

Music by Harold Arlen

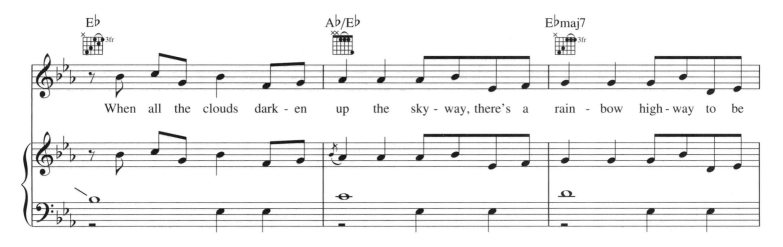

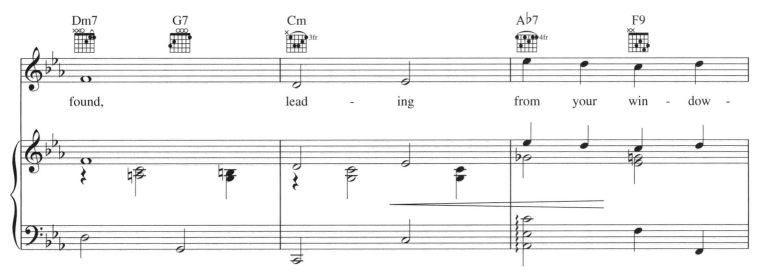

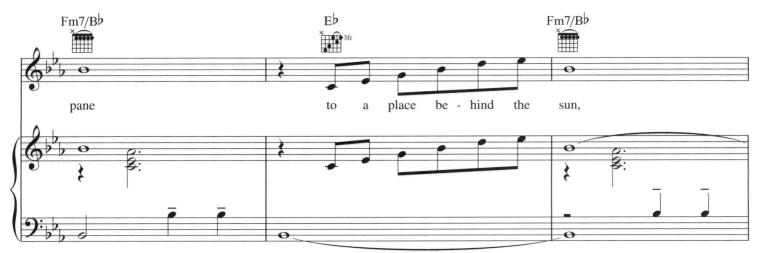

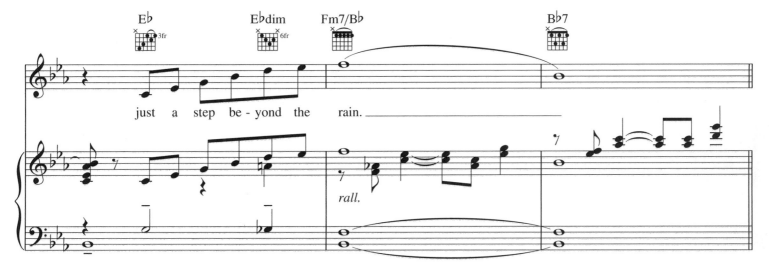

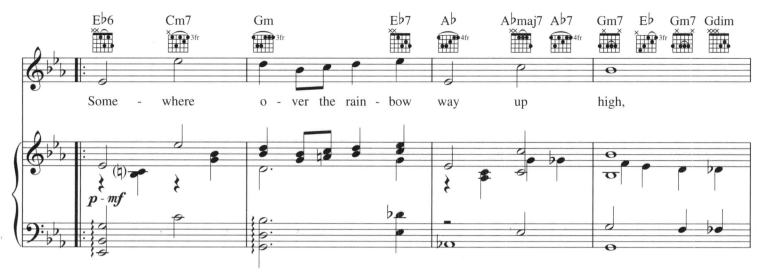

Some-where o-ver the rain-bow way up high,

there's a land that I heard of once in a lull-a-

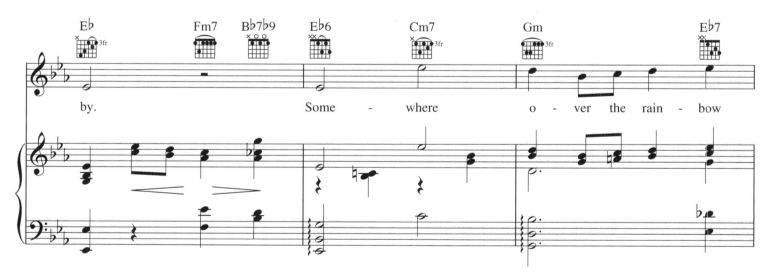

by. Some-where o-ver the rain-bow

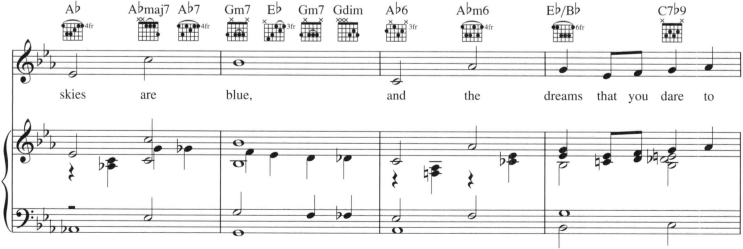

skies are blue, and the dreams that you dare to

fly.　Birds　fly　o - ver the rain - bow,　why then, oh why can't

I?　　I?

If

hap - py lit - tle blue-birds fly be - yond the rain - bow, why oh why can't　I? _____

Pieces of Dreams
(Little Boy Lost)
from the Motion Picture PIECES OF DREAMS

Lyrics by
Alan and Marilyn Bergman

Music by Michel Legrand

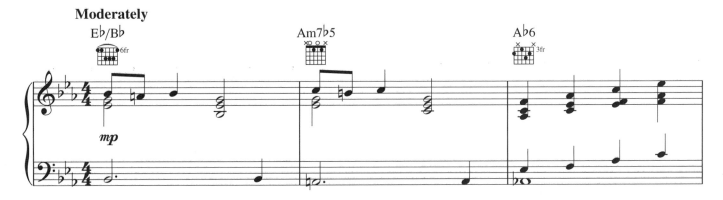

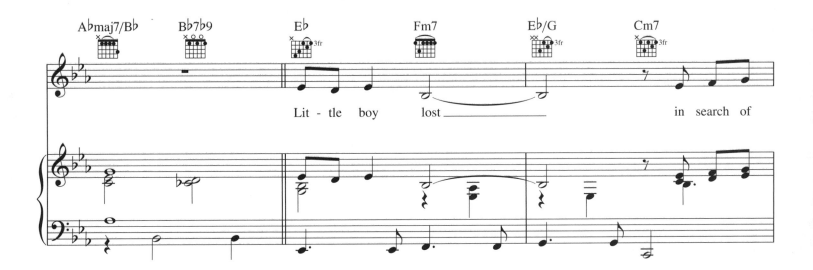

Lit - tle boy lost _____ in search of

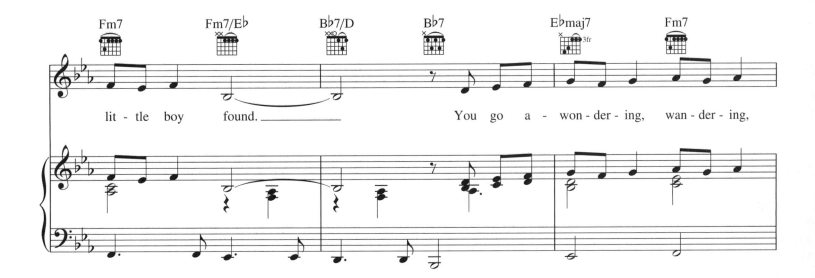

lit - tle boy found. _____ You go a - won - der - ing, wan - der - ing,

stum - bl - ing, tum - bl - ing, round! Round!

When will you find _____ what's on the tip of your mind? _____

_____ Why are you blind _____ to all you

ev - er were, nev - er were, real - ly are, near - ly are? Lit - tle boy false _____

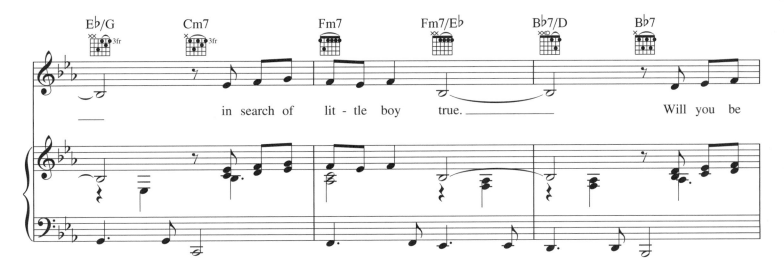

in search of lit-tle boy true. _____ Will you be

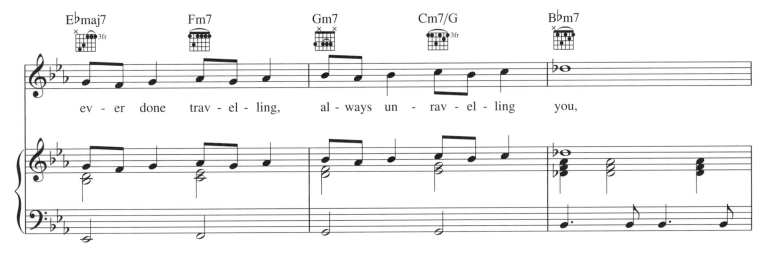

ev-er done trav-el-ling, al-ways un-rav-el-ling you,

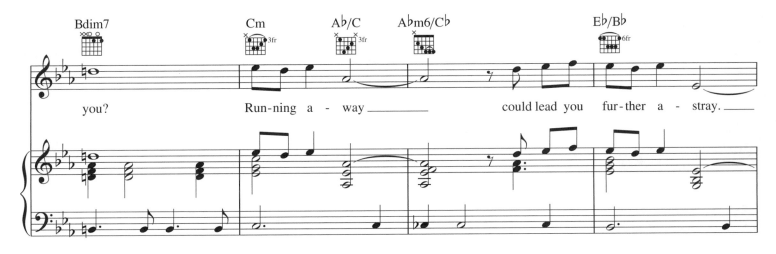

you? Run-ning a-way _____ could lead you fur-ther a-stray. _____

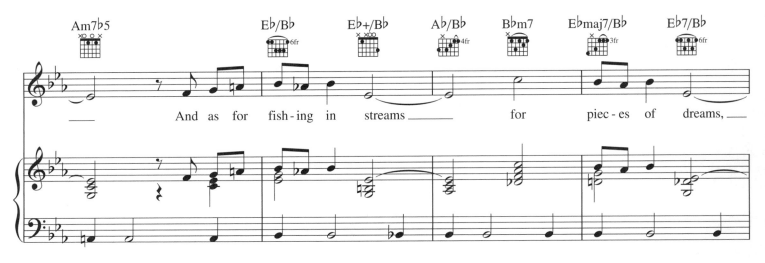

And as for fish-ing in streams _____ for piec-es of dreams, _____

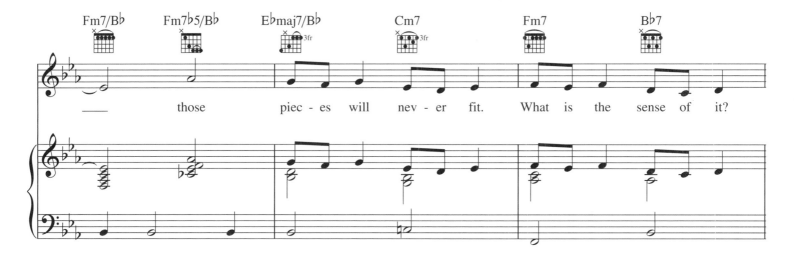

those piec-es will nev-er fit. What is the sense of it?

Lit-tle boy blue, _____ don't let your lit-tle sheep roam. _____

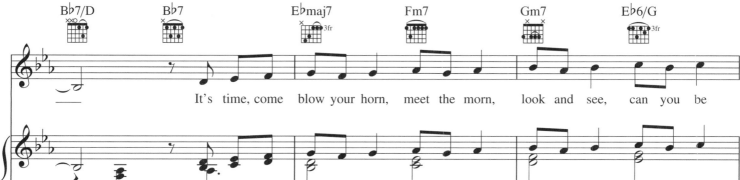

It's time, come blow your horn, meet the morn, look and see, can you be

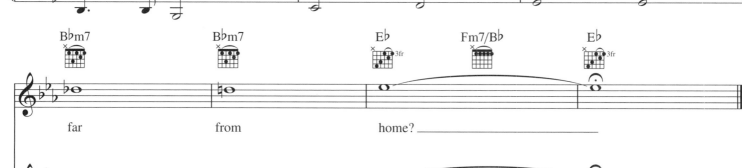

far from home? _____

Puttin' On the Ritz

from the Motion Picture PUTTIN' ON THE RITZ

Words and Music by
Irving Berlin

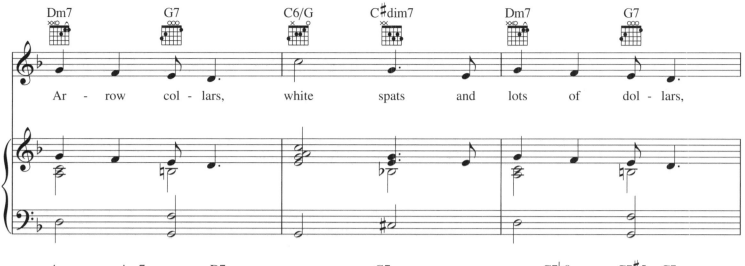

like an Eng - lish chap - pie, ___ ver - y snap - py.
look like Gar - y Coo - per, ___ su - per du - per.)

Come, let's mix where Rock - e - fel - lers walk with sticks or "um - ber -

el - las" in their mitts, _____ put - tin' on the

Ritz. _____

Ritz. _____

Que Sera, Sera

(Whatever Will Be, Will Be)

from THE MAN WHO KNEW TOO MUCH

Words and Music by
Jay Livingston and Raymond B. Evans

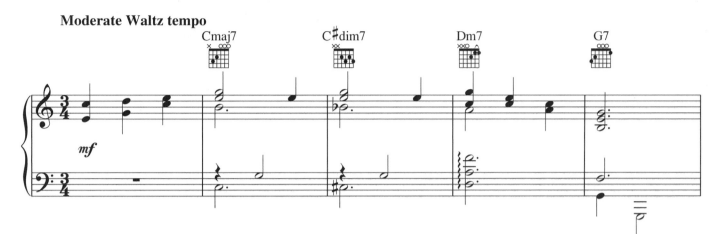

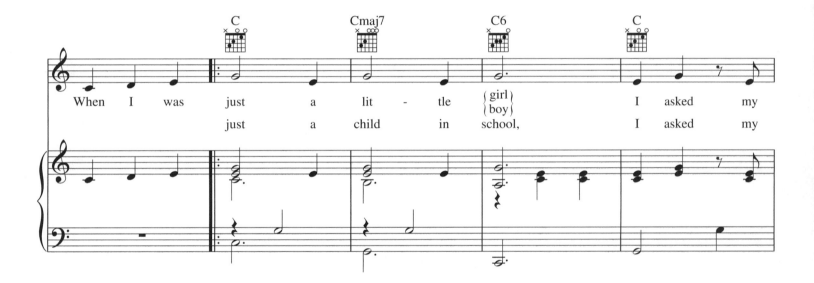

When I was just a lit - tle {girl/boy} I asked my

just a child in school, I asked my

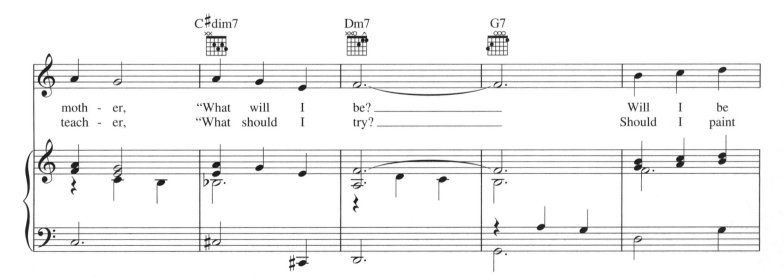

moth - er, "What will I be? _____ Will I be

teach - er, "What should I try? _____ Should I paint

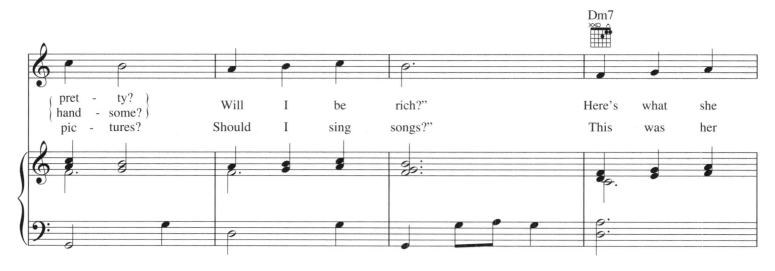

{ pret - ty? }
{ hand - some? }
pic - tures? Should I sing songs?"

Will I be rich?"

Here's what she
This was her

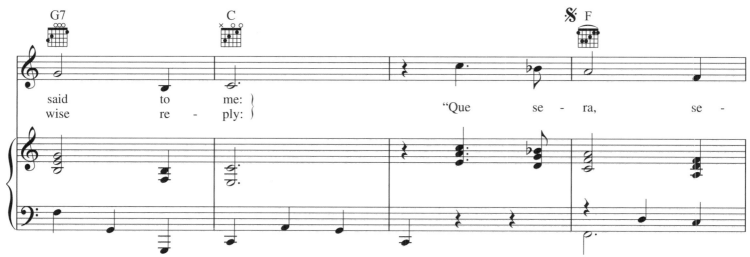

said to me: }
wise re - ply: }

"Que se - ra, se -

ra, _____ What - ev - er will be will be. _____

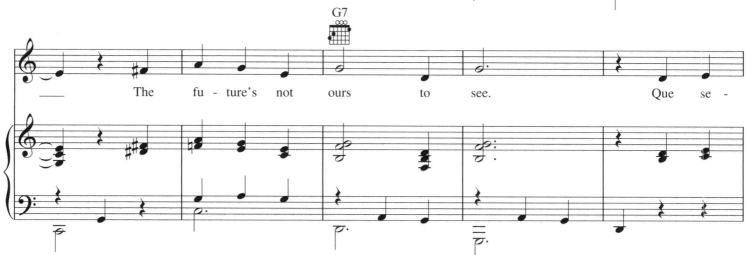

The fu - ture's not ours to see. Que se -

233

ra, se - ra! _____ What will be will

be!" _____ When I was ___

When I grew up and fell in love,
Now I have chil - dren of my own,

I asked my {lov - er,
          {sweet - heart,} "What lies a - head? _____
they ask their {moth - er,
               {fa - ther,} "What will I be? _____

Raindrops Keep Fallin' on My Head

from BUTCH CASSIDY AND THE SUNDANCE KID

Lyric by Hal David

Music by Burt Bacharach

sun. And I said I did-n't like the way he got things done. Sleep-in'on the

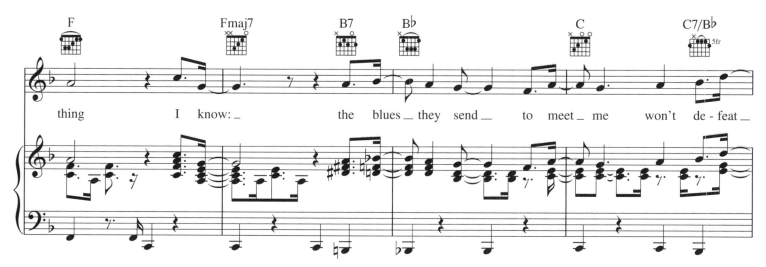

job. Those rain - drops are fall - in'on my head. They keep fall - in'! But there's one

thing I know: _ the blues _ they send _ to meet _ me won't de - feat _

___ me. It won't be long ___ till hap - pi - ness ___ steps up ___

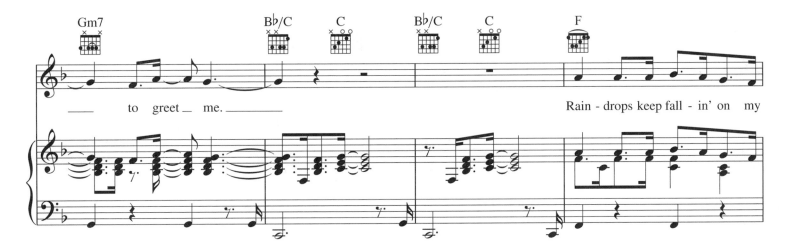

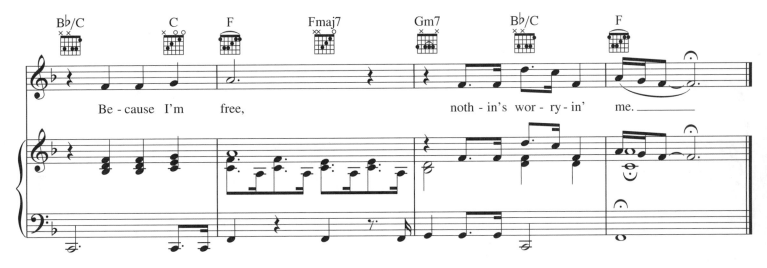

238

The Rose

from the Twentieth Century-Fox Motion Picture Release THE ROSE

Words and Music by
Amanda McBroom

love, it is a flow - er, and you, its on - ly seed. _____

It's the ___ heart a - fraid of break - ing that
night has been too lone - ly and the

nev - er _____ learns to __ dance. It's the __ dream _____ a - fraid of wak - ing that
road _____ has been too _ long, and you _ think _____ that love is on - ly for the

nev - er _____ takes the _____ chance. It's the __ one _____ who won't
luck - y _____ and the _____ strong, just re - mem - ber _____ in the

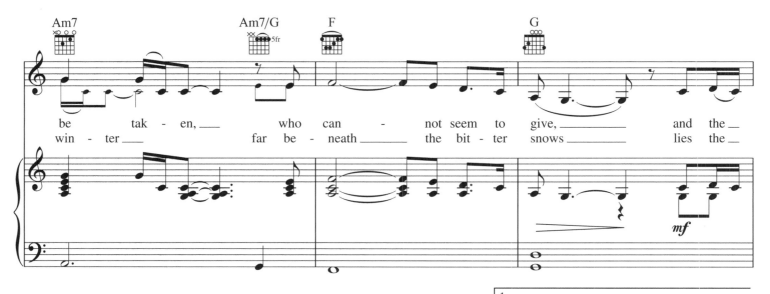

be tak - en, ___ who can - not seem to give, _____ and the _

win - ter ___ far be - neath _____ the bit - ter snows _____ lies the _

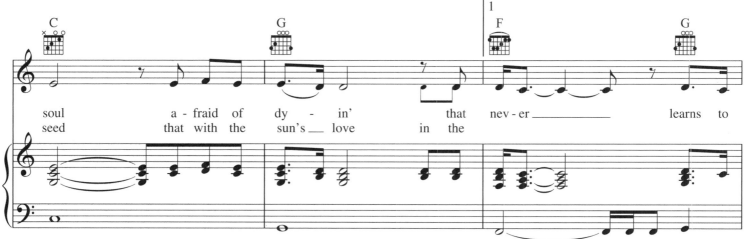

soul a - fraid of dy - in' that nev - er _____ learns to

seed that with the sun's _ love in the

live. _____ When the _ spring be - comes the

rose.

(Vocal 1st time only)

The Second Time Around

from HIGH TIME

Words and Music by
Sammy Cahn and James Van Heusen

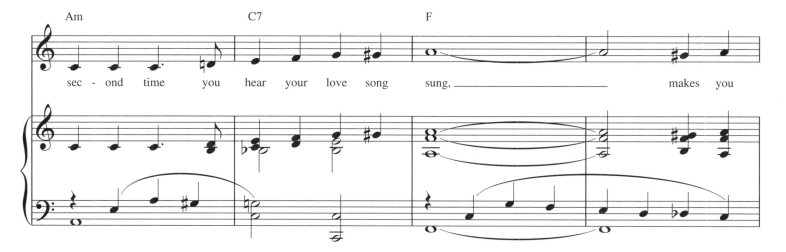

Am   C7   F

sec - ond time you hear your love song sung, _____ makes you

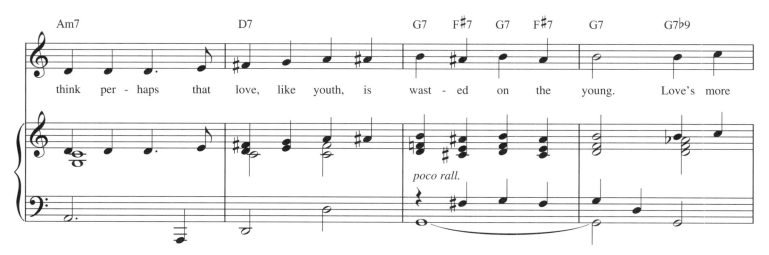

Am7   D7   G7 F#7 G7 F#7 G7   G7b9

think per - haps that love, like youth, is wast - ed on the young. Love's more

poco rall.

C   C/E   Eb°7   Dm   Dm(maj7) Dm7   G13   G7b9

comf' - ta - ble the sec - ond time you fall, _____ like a

a tempo

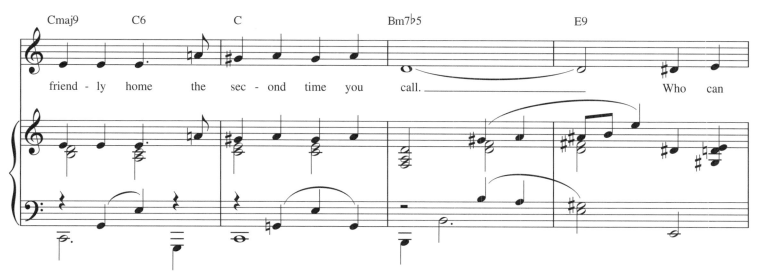

Cmaj9   C6   C   Bm7b5   E9

friend - ly home the sec - ond time you call. _____ Who can

Singin' in the Rain

from SINGIN' IN THE RAIN

Lyric by Arthur Freed

Music by Nacio Herb Brown

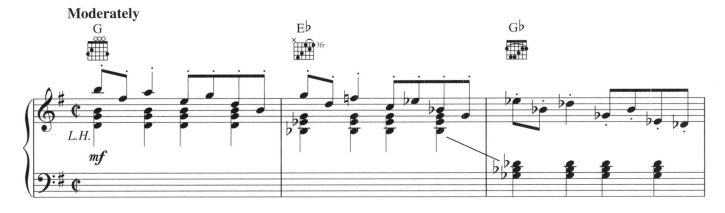

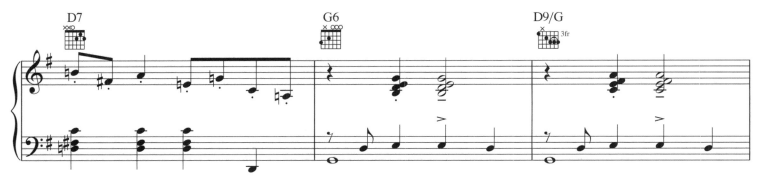

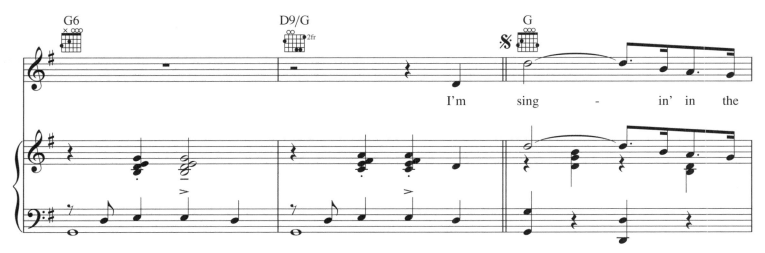

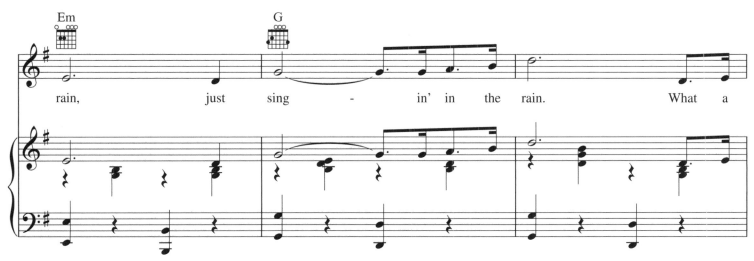

glo - ri - ous feel - ing I'm hap - py a -

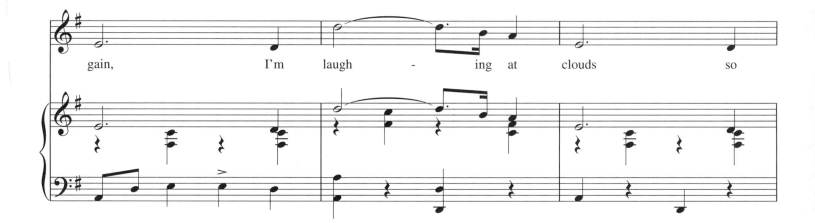

gain, I'm laugh - ing at clouds so

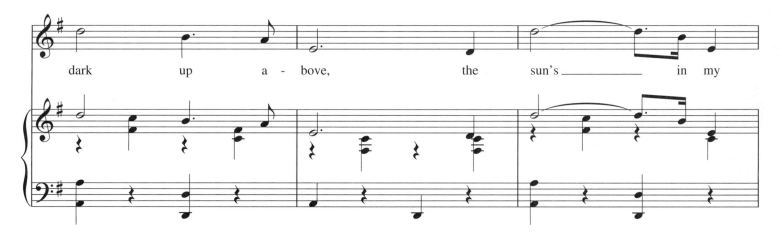

dark up a - bove, the sun's _____ in my

heart _____ and I'm read - y for love. Let the

246

storm - y clouds chase ev - 'ry - one _____ from the

place. Come on _____ with the rain, I've a

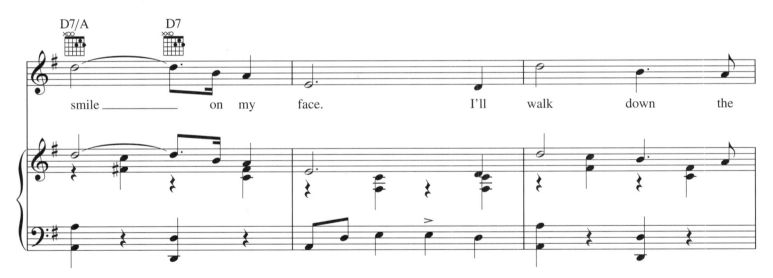

smile _____ on my face. I'll walk down the

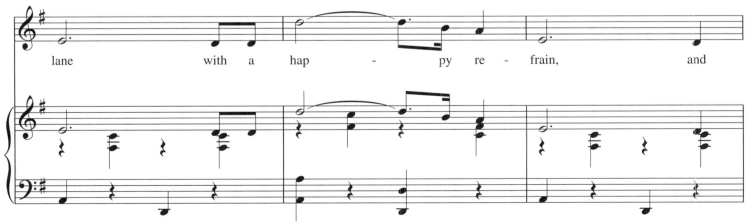

lane with a hap - py re - frain, and

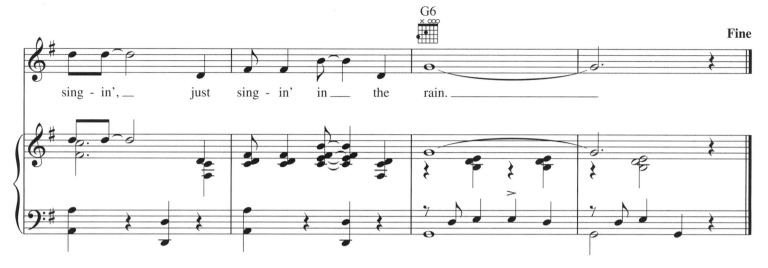

Fine

sing - in', __ just sing - in' in __ the rain. _____

Why am I smil - in' and why do I sing? __

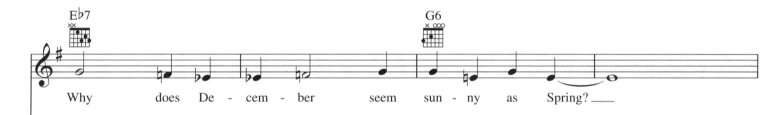

Why does De - cem - ber seem sun - ny as Spring? __

Why do I get up each morn - ing to start __

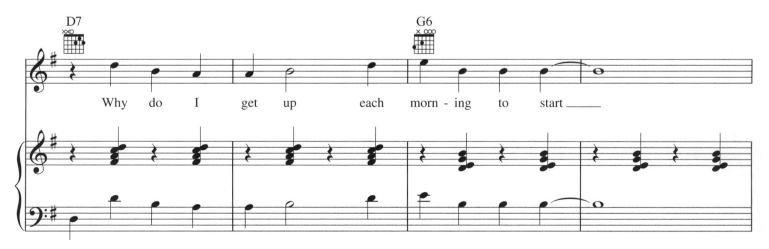

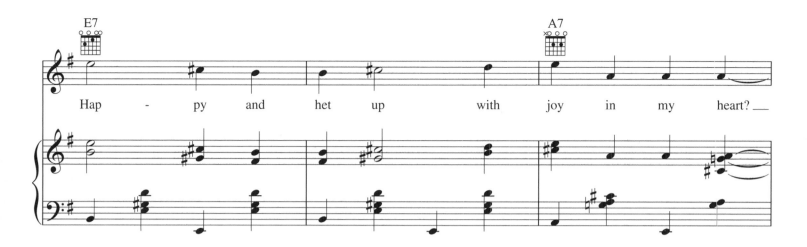

Hap - py and het up with joy in my heart? __

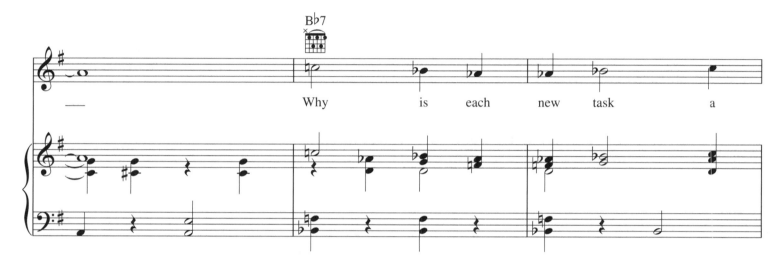

__ Why is each new task a

tri - fle to do? _____ Be - cause I am

D.S. al Fine

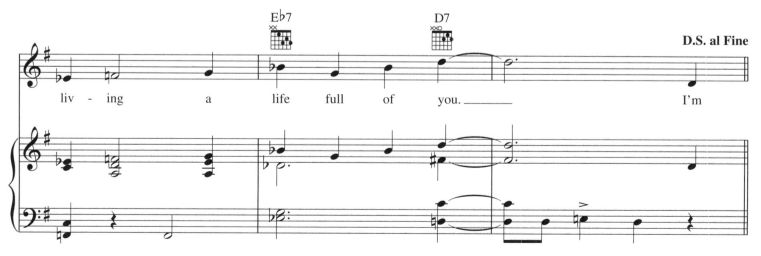

liv - ing a life full of you. ____ I'm

Secret Love
from CALAMITY JANE

Words by Paul Francis Webster

Music by Sammy Fain

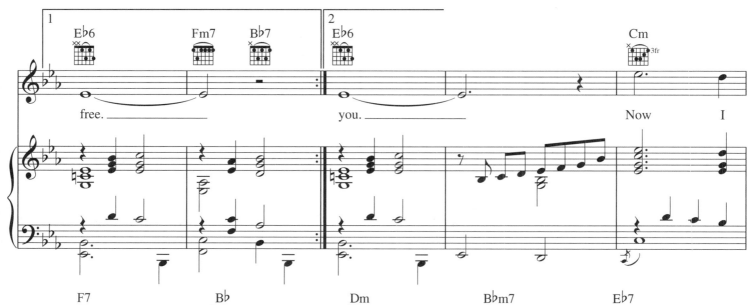

free. _____ you. _____ Now I

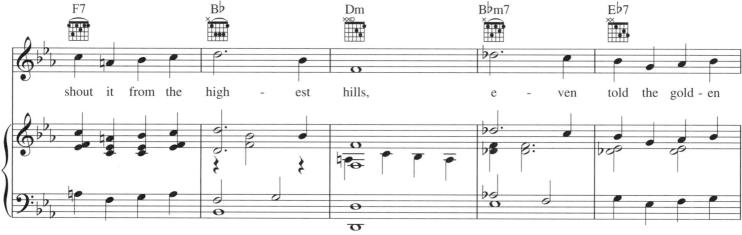

shout it from the high - est hills, e - ven told the gold - en

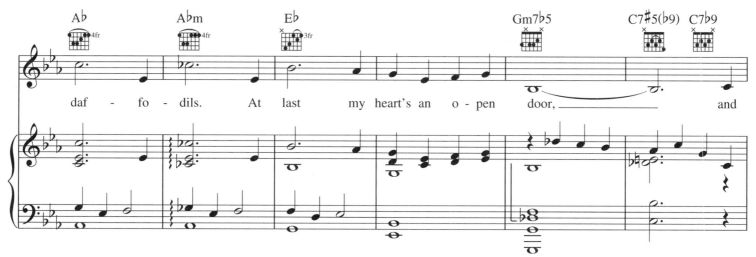

daf - fo - dils. At last my heart's an o - pen door, _____ and

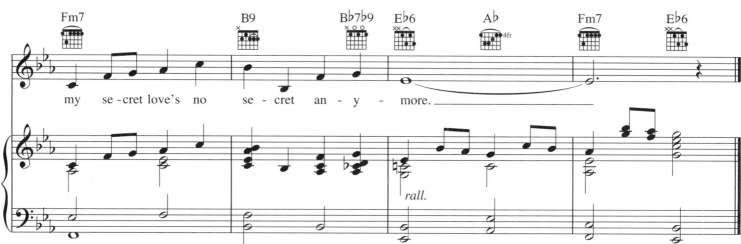

my se - cret love's no se - cret an - y - more. _____

rall.

Sisters

from the Motion Picture Irving Berlin's WHITE CHRISTMAS

Words and Music by
Irving Berlin

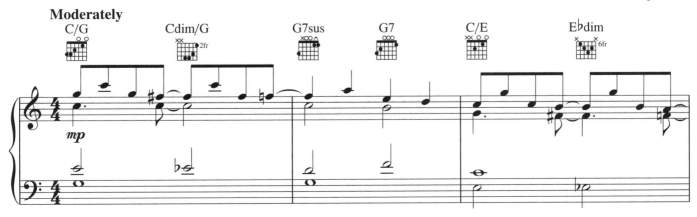

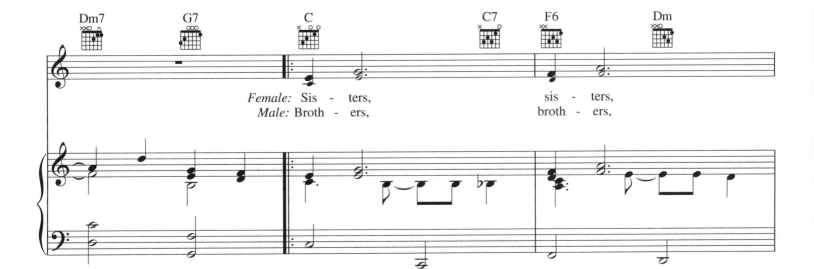

Female: Sis - ters,   sis - ters,
Male: Broth - ers,   broth - ers,

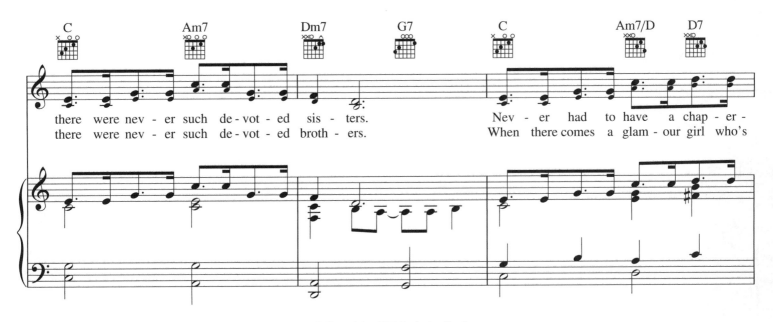

there were nev - er such de - vot - ed sis - ters.   Nev - er had to have a chap - er -
there were nev - er such de - vot - ed broth - ers.   When there comes a glam - our girl who's

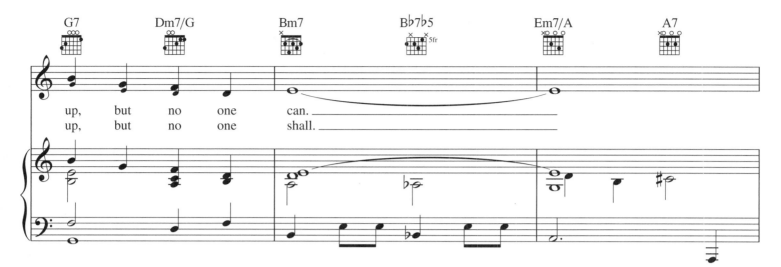

up, but no one can. _____
up, but no one shall. _____

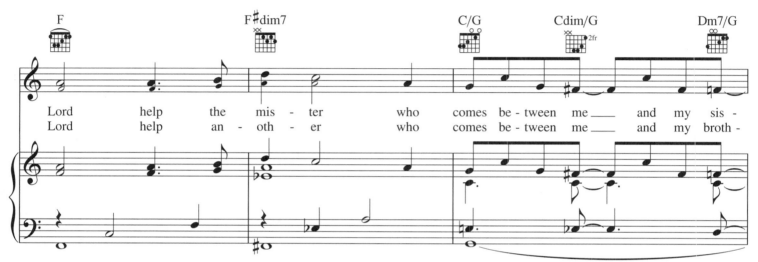

Lord help the mis - ter who comes be - tween me ____ and my sis -
Lord help an - oth - er who comes be - tween me ____ and my broth -

- ter. And Lord help the sis - ter who
- er. And Lord help the broth - er who

comes be - tween me ____ and my man. man.
comes be - tween me ____ and my gal. gal.

Somewhere in My Memory

from the Twentieth Century Fox Motion Picture HOME ALONE

Words by Leslie Bricusse

Music by John Williams

Gently and with simplicity

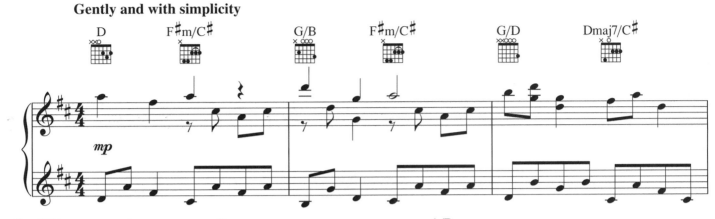

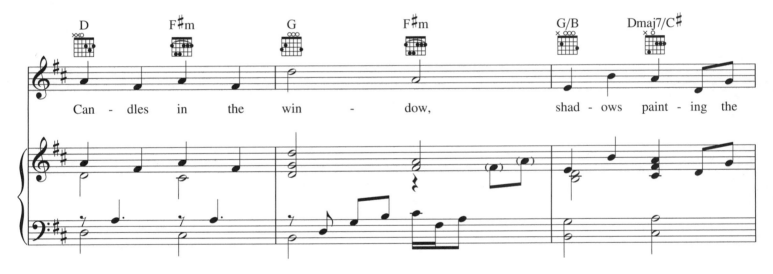

Can - dles in the win - dow, shad - ows paint - ing the

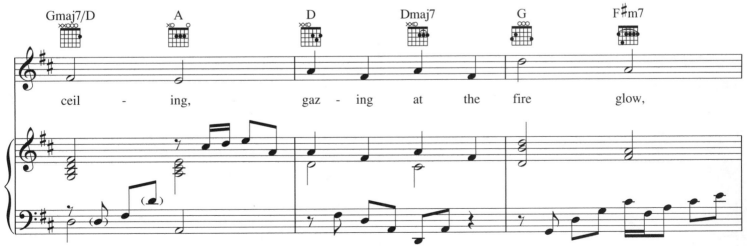

ceil - ing, gaz - ing at the fire glow,

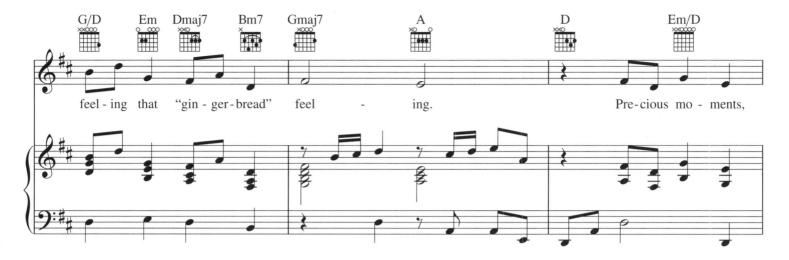

feel - ing that "gin - ger - bread" feel - ing. Pre - cious mo - ments,

spe - cial peo - ple, hap - py fac - es I can see.

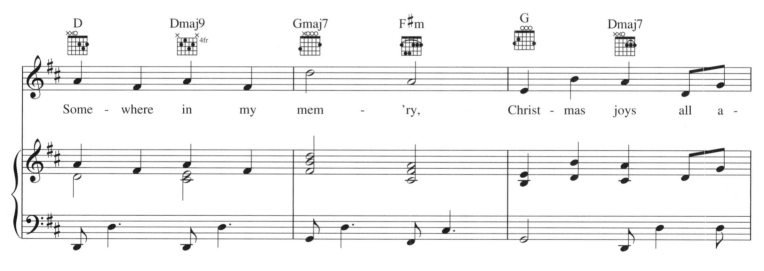

Some - where in my mem - 'ry, Christ - mas joys all a -

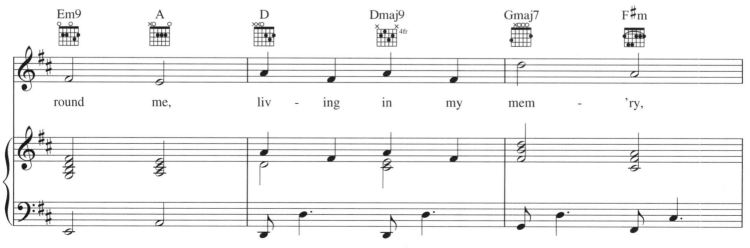

round me, liv - ing in my mem - 'ry,

all of the mu - sic,   all of the mag - ic,   all of the fam - 'ly

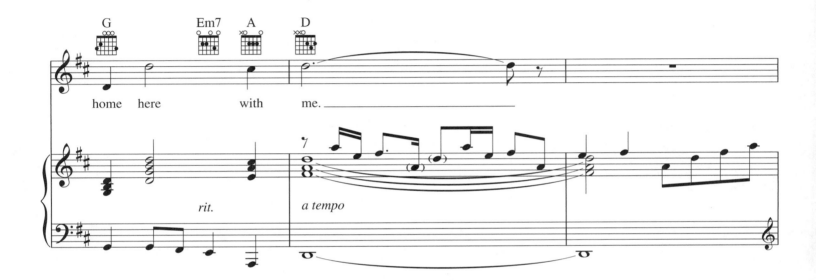

home here   with   me. _____

rit.   *a tempo*

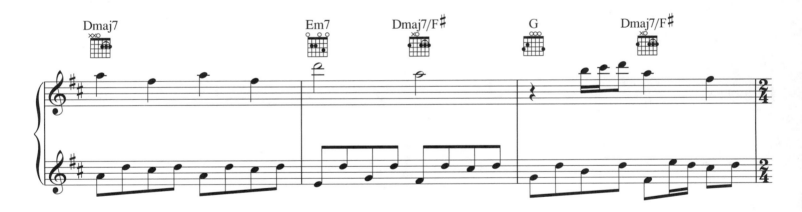

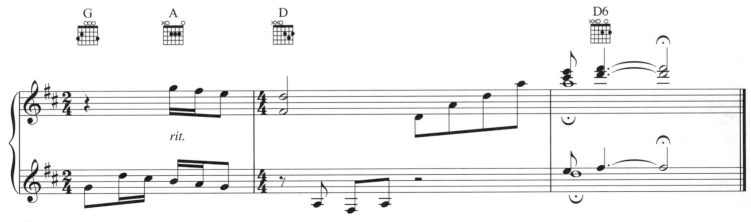

rit.

Somewhere, My Love

Lara's Theme from DOCTOR ZHIVAGO

Lyric by Paul Francis Webster

Music by Maurice Jarre

Moderately, with expression

Some - where, my love, there will be songs to sing,

al - though the snow cov - ers the hope of spring.

Some - where a hill blos - soms in green and gold,

warm as the wind, soft as the kiss of snow.

Till then, my sweet, think of me now and then.
(Lar - a, my own)

God - speed, my love, 'til you are mine a - gain.

'til you are mine _____ a - gain. _____

rit.

Stand by Me

featured in the Motion Picture STAND BY ME

Words and Music by
Jerry Leiber, Mike Stoller
and Ben E. King

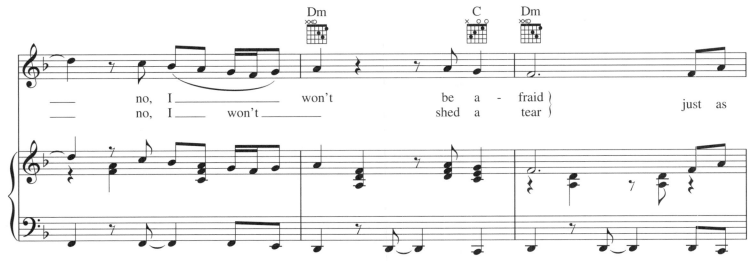

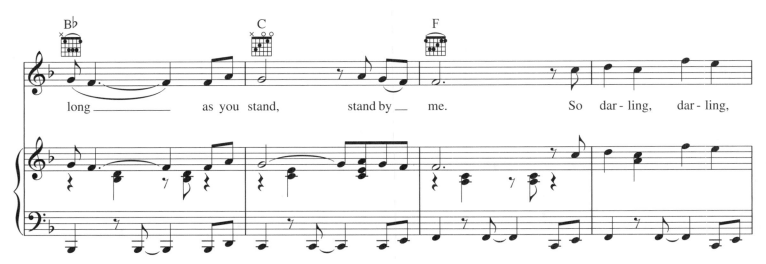

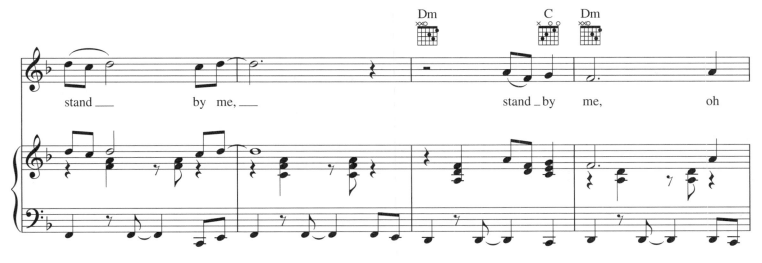

stand, _____ stand by __ me, stand by __ me.

If the Dar-ling, stand _____ by me,

stand by me, oh stand, _____

Repeat and Fade

stand by __ me, stand by __ me. When-ev-er I'm in trou-ble, won't you

Star Wars
(Main Theme)
from STAR WARS, THE EMPIRE STRIKES BACK and RETURN OF THE JEDI

Music by
JOHN WILLIAMS

Majestically, steady March (♩ = 108)

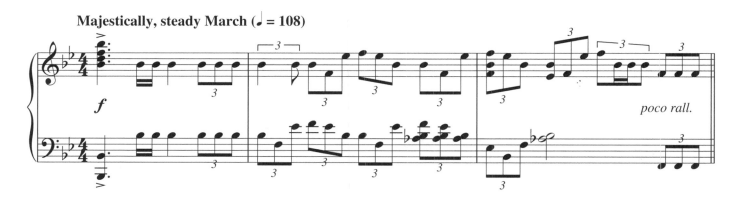

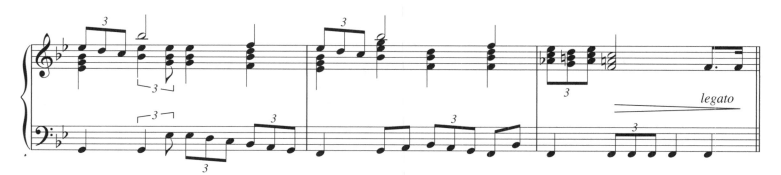

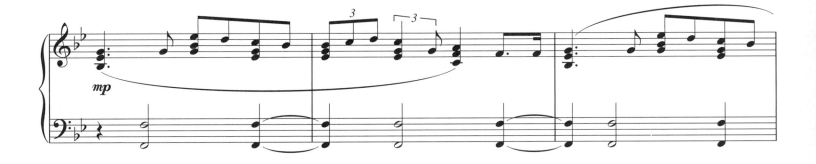

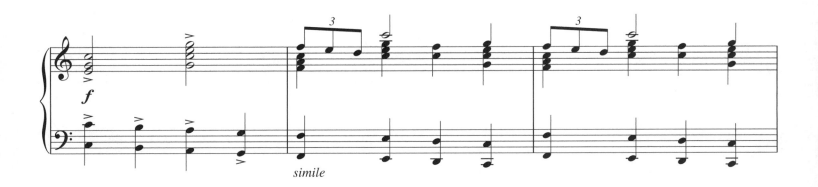

Summer Nights

from GREASE

Lyric and Music by
Warren Casey and Jim Jacobs

Shu-da bop bop. Shu-da bop bop. *Girl:* He got friend-ly, hold-ing my hand. ___ *Boy:* She got friend-ly,

down in the sand. _____ *Girl:* He was sweet; just turned eight-een. ___ *Boy:* She was good. You

know what I mean. _ *Both:* Sum-mer heat; boy and girl meet. ___ But, _ uh, oh those sum-mer nights. _

Girls: Tell me more. Tell me more. How much dough did he spend? _

(Theme from)
A Summer Place
from A SUMMER PLACE

Words by
Mack Discant

Music by
Max Steiner

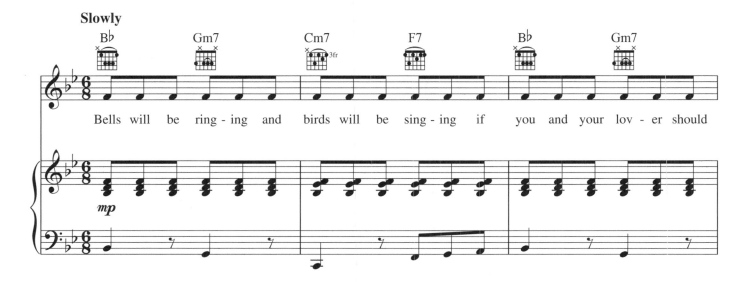

Bells will be ring-ing and birds will be sing-ing if you and your lov-er should

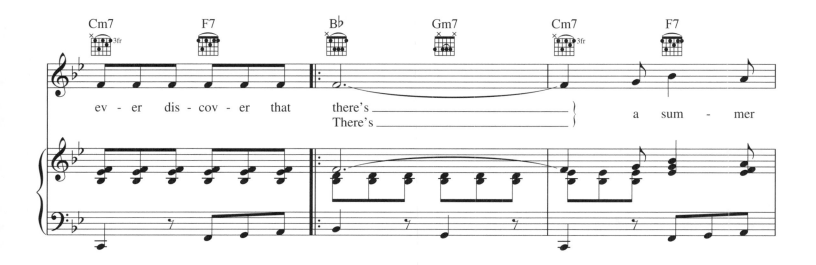

ev-er dis-cov-er that there's _____ / There's _____ a sum-mer

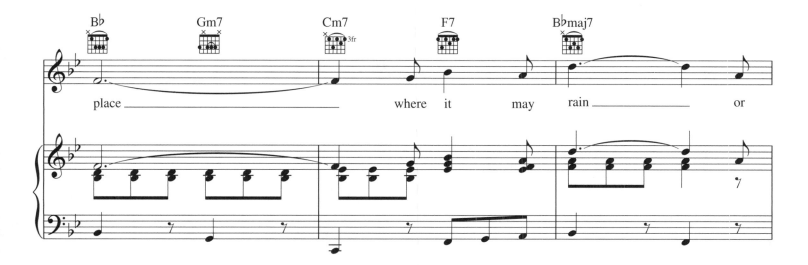

place _____ where it may rain _____ or

storm. _____ Yet I'm safe _____ and warm. _____ For with -

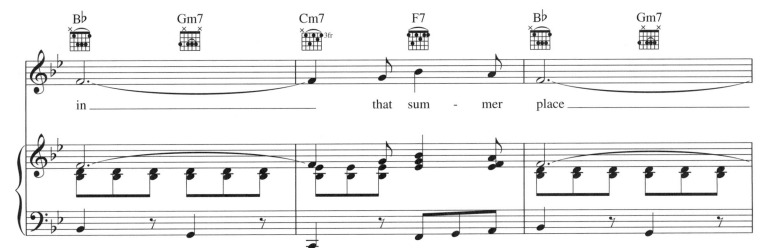

in _____ that sum - mer place _____

_____ your arms reach out _____ to me _____ and my

heart _____ is free _____ from all care. _____

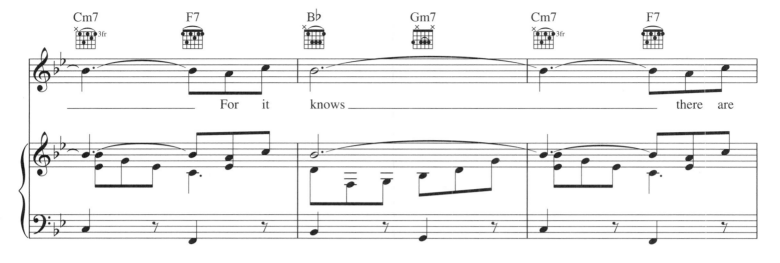

For it knows _____ there are

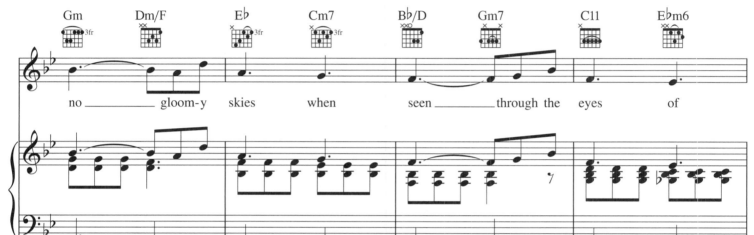

no _____ gloom-y skies when seen _____ through the eyes of

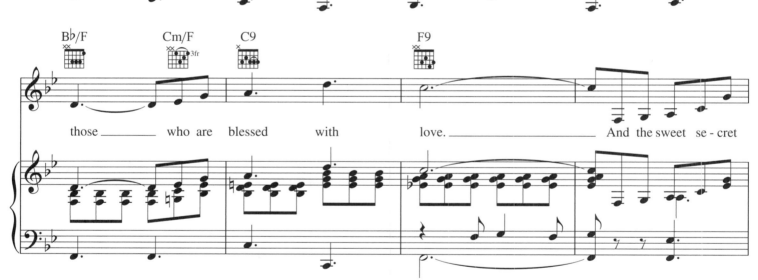

those _____ who are blessed with love. _____ And the sweet se - cret

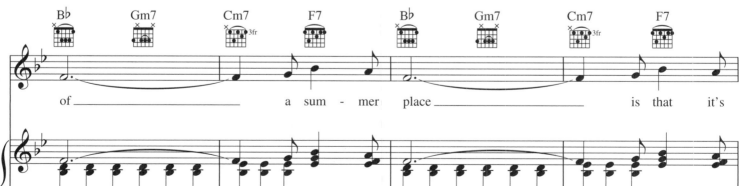

of _____ a sum - mer place _____ is that it's

275

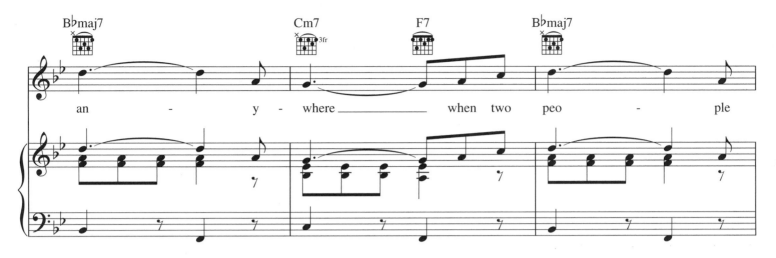

an - y - where _____ when two peo - ple

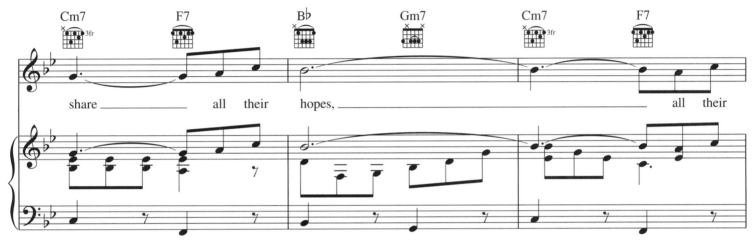

share _____ all their hopes, _____ all their

dreams, _____ all their love. _____

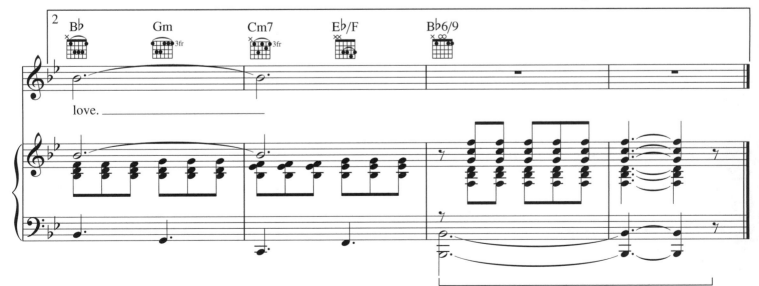

love. _____

276

That's Amoré

(That's Love)

from the Paramount Picture THE CADDY

Words by Jack Brooks

Music by Harry Warren

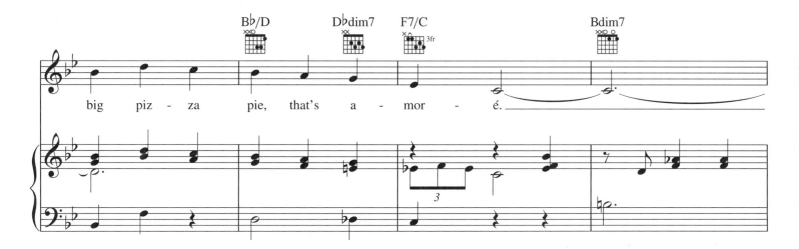

big piz - za pie, that's a - mor - é. _____

___ When the world seems to shine like you've had too much

wine, that's a - mor - é. _____ Bells will

ring, ting - a - ling - a - ling, ting - a - ling - a - ling, and you'll sing, "Vee - ta

bel - la." _____ Hearts will

play, tip-py-tip-py - tay, tip-py-tip-py - tay like a gay tar-an -

tel - la. _____ (Luck-y fel - la.) When the

stars make you drool just like pas-ta fa - zool, that's a-

mor - é. When you dance down the street with a cloud at your feet, you're in love. When you walk in a dream but you know you're not dream-ing, Sig -

F7/C   Bdim7   Cm7   F7

D7/A   A♭7♭5   G7

Cm   E♭m6

nor - é, _____ scuz - za

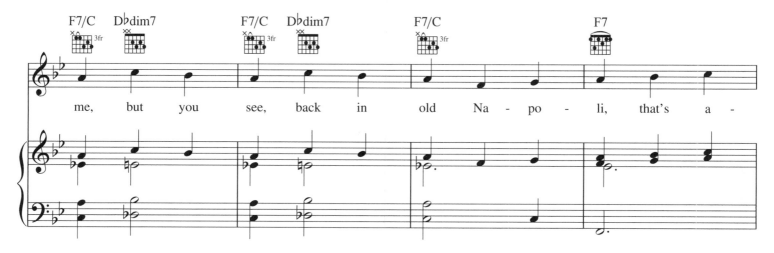

me, but you see, back in old Na - po - li, that's a -

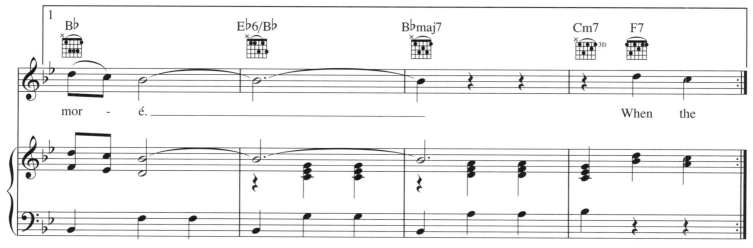

mor - é. _____ When the

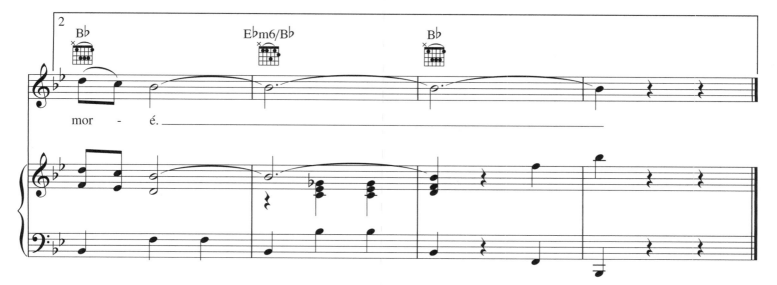

mor - é. _____

Tara's Theme
(My Own True Love)
from GONE WITH THE WIND

By Max Steiner

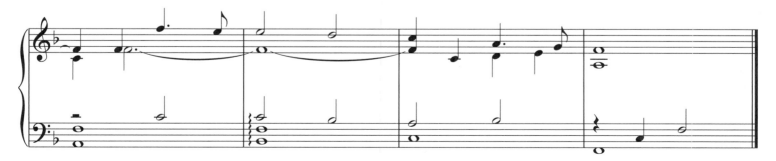

A Time for Us

(Love Theme)

from the Paramount Picture ROMEO AND JULIET

Words by
Larry Kusik and Eddie Snyder

Music by Nino Rota

Slowly and expressively

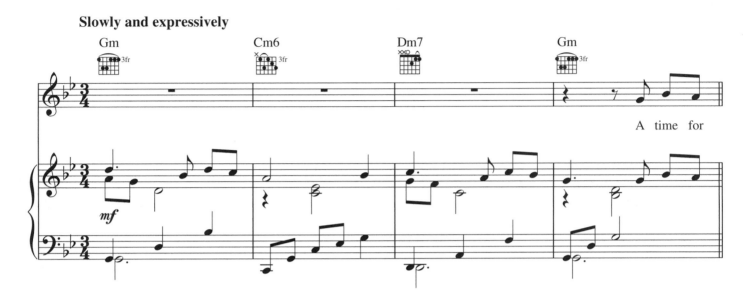

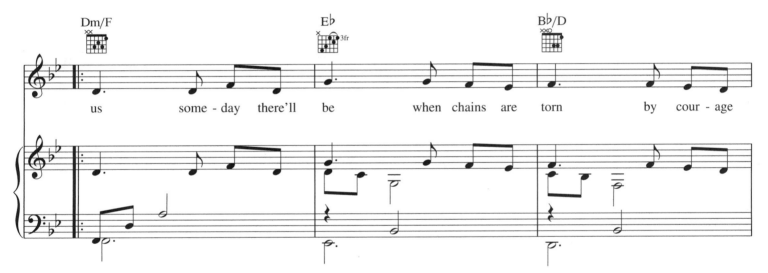

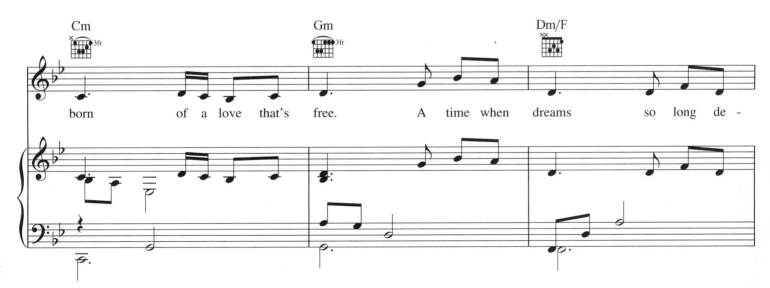

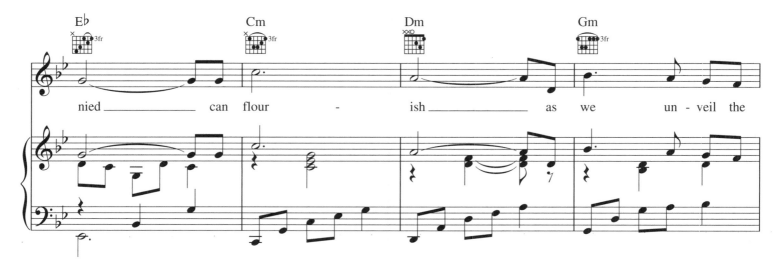

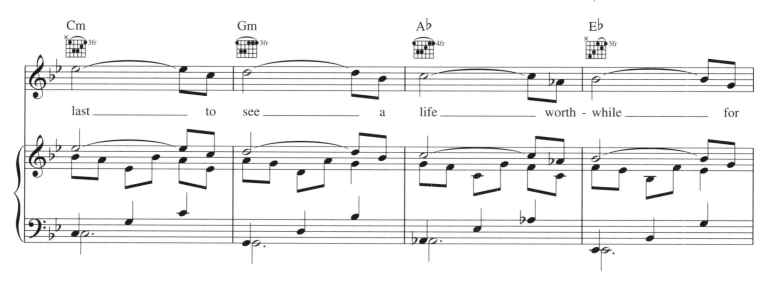

The Trolley Song

from MEET ME IN ST. LOUIS

Words and Music by
Hugh Martin and Ralph Blane

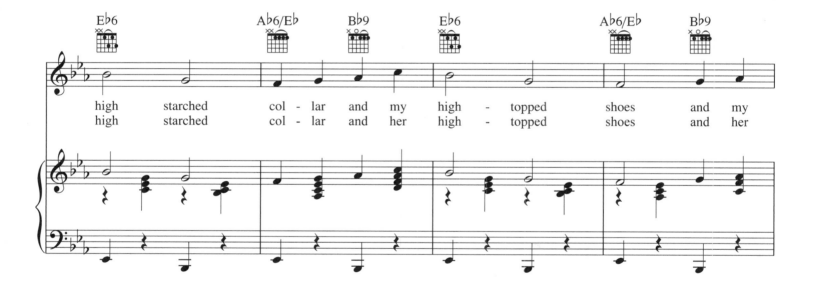

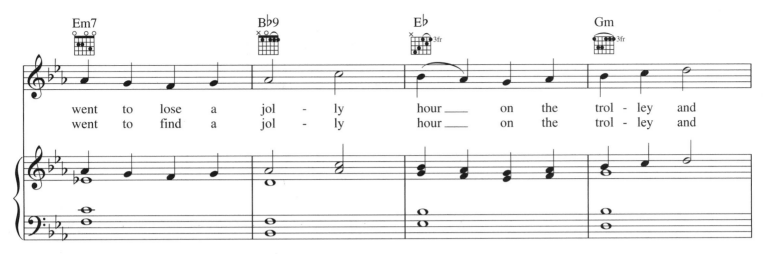

went to lose a jol - ly hour ___ on the trol - ley and
went to find a jol - ly hour ___ on the trol - ley and

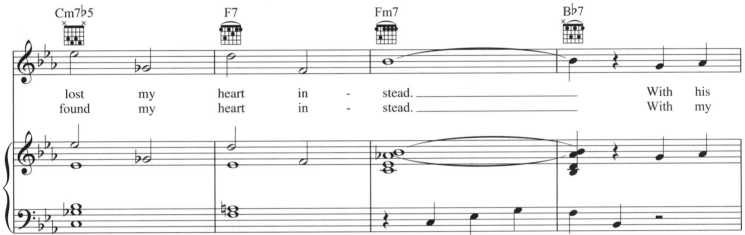

lost my heart in - stead. _____ With his
found my heart in - stead. _____ With my

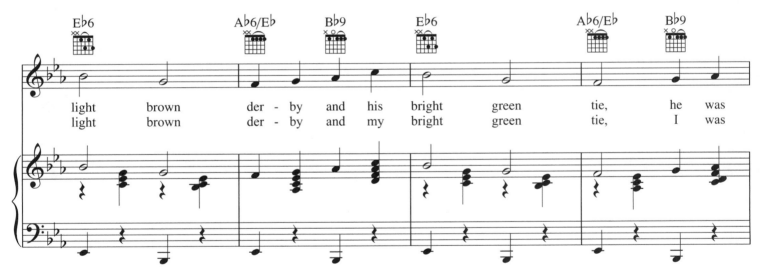

light brown der - by and his bright green tie, he was
light brown der - by and my bright green tie, I was

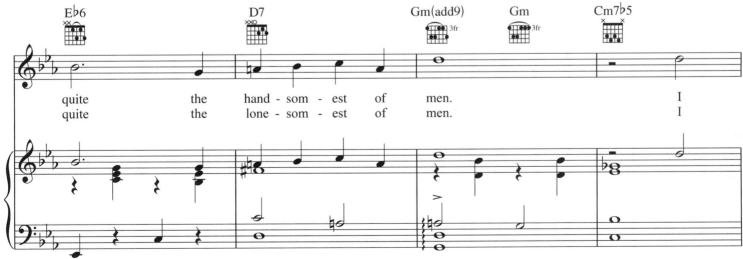

quite the hand - som - est of men. I
quite the lone - som - est of men. I

288

start - ed to yen, so I count - ed to ten, then I
start - ed to yen, so I count - ed to ten, then I

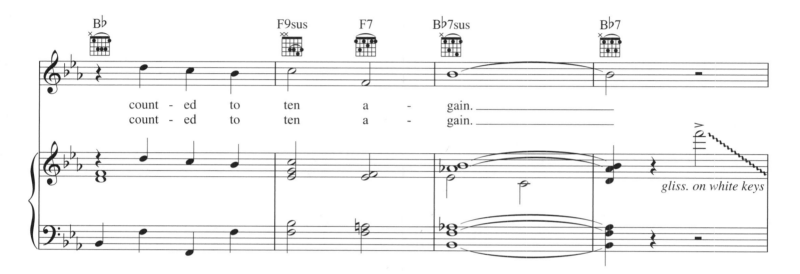

count - ed to ten a - gain.
count - ed to ten a - gain.

gliss. on white keys

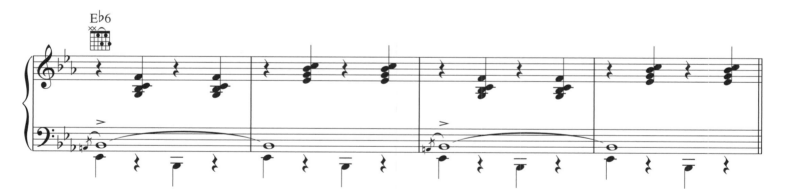

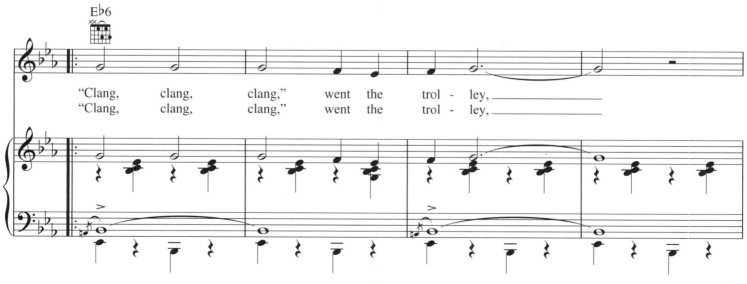

"Clang, clang, clang," went the trol - ley, ___
"Clang, clang, clang," went the trol - ley, ___

293

feels _____ when the un - i - verse
feels _____ when the un - i - verse

reels. _____
reels. _____

start - ed to leave I took hold of his sleeve with my
start - ed to leave I took hold of her sleeve with my

hand. _____ And as if it were
hand. _____ And as if it were

Up Where We Belong

from the Paramount Picture AN OFFICER AND A GENTLEMAN

Words by Will Jennings

Music by
Buffy Sainte-Marie and Jack Nitzsche

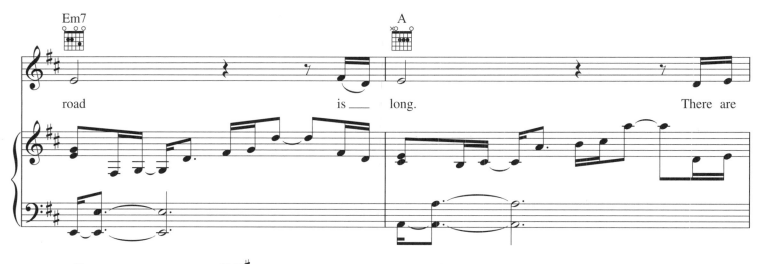

road   is — long.   There are

moun - tains — in our — way, —   but we

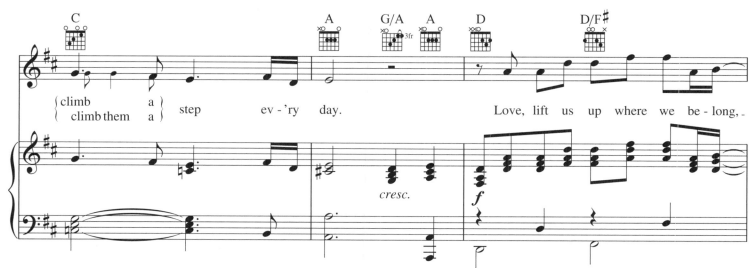

{ climb   a }
{ climb them a } step ev -'ry day.   Love, lift us up where we be - long, _

cresc.   *f*

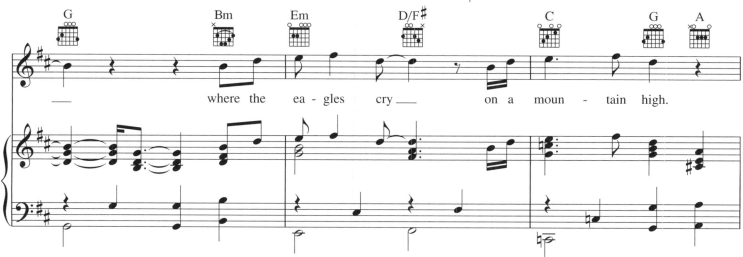

where the ea - gles cry — on a moun - tain high.

Love, lift us up where we be-long, _____ far from the

world we know; ___ up where the clear winds blow. ___

clear winds blow. ___ Time goes by, ___

no time to cry, _____ life's you and I, ___ a - live, ___ to - day. ___

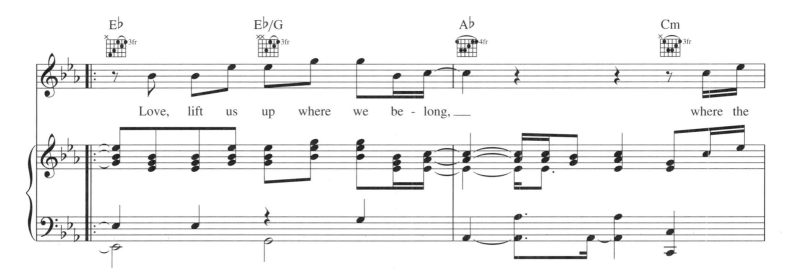

Love, lift us up where we be - long, ___ where the

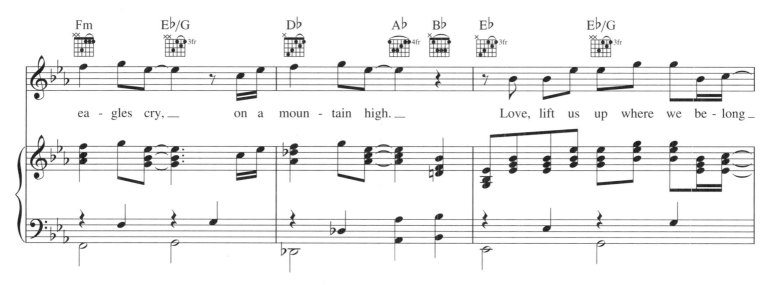

ea - gles cry, ___ on a moun - tain high. ___ Love, lift us up where we be - long ___

Repeat and Fade

___ far from the world we know; ___ where the clear winds blow. ___

Optional Ending

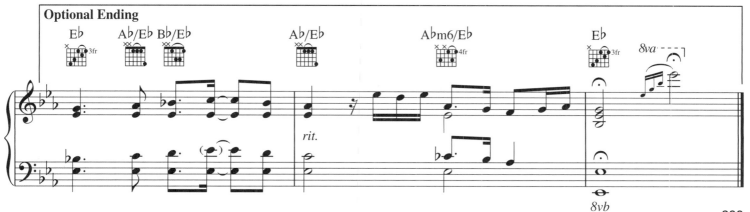

rit.

The Way We Were

from the Motion Picture THE WAY WE WERE

Words by
Alan and Marilyn Bergman

Music by Marvin Hamlisch

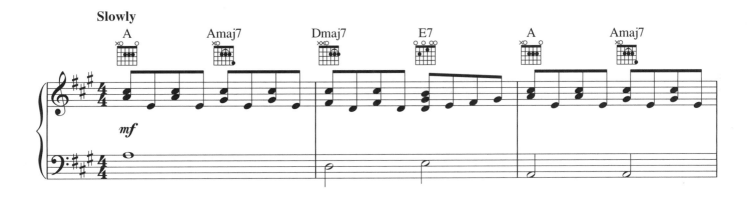

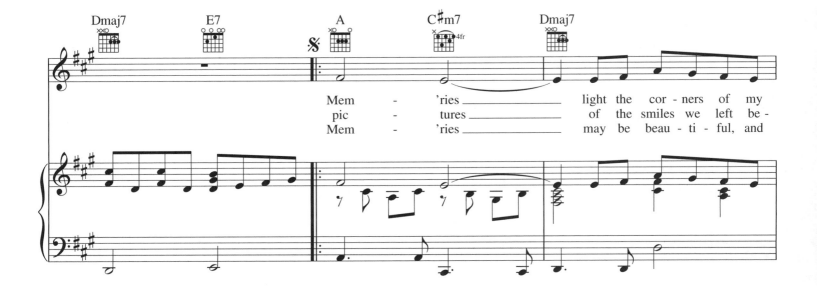

Mem - 'ries _____ light the cor - ners of my
pic - tures _____ of the smiles we left be -
Mem - 'ries _____ may be beau - ti - ful, and

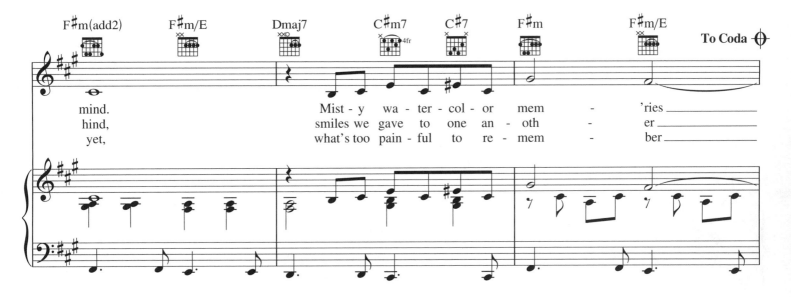

mind.
hind,   Mist - y wa - ter - col - or mem - 'ries _____
yet,   smiles we gave to one an - oth - er _____
         what's too pain - ful to re - mem - ber _____

To Coda ⊕

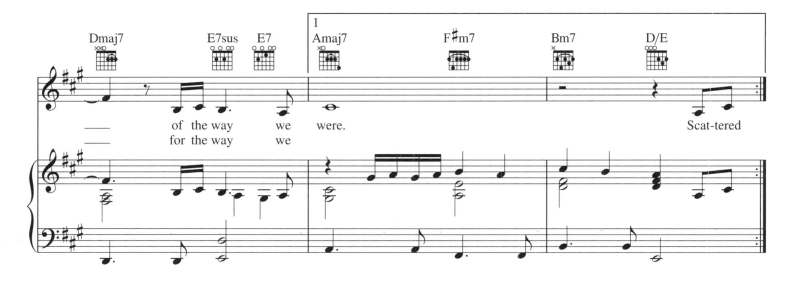

of the way we were.
for the way we
Scat-tered

were. _____
Can it be that it was all so sim-ple then,

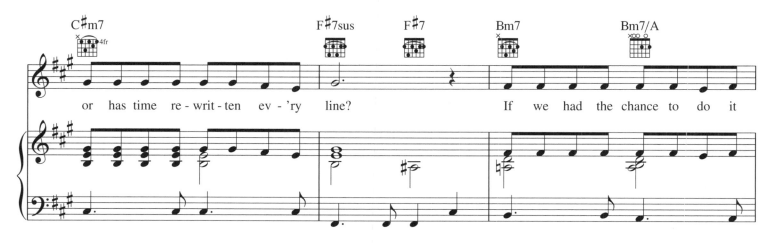

or has time re-writ-ten ev-'ry line?
If we had the chance to do it

all a-gain, tell me would we? __
Could we? __

D.S. al Coda

301

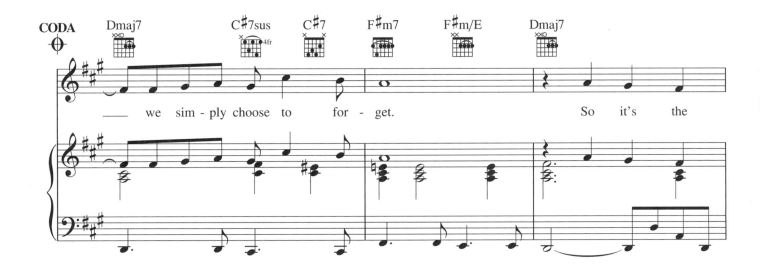

CODA

we sim-ply choose to for-get. So it's the

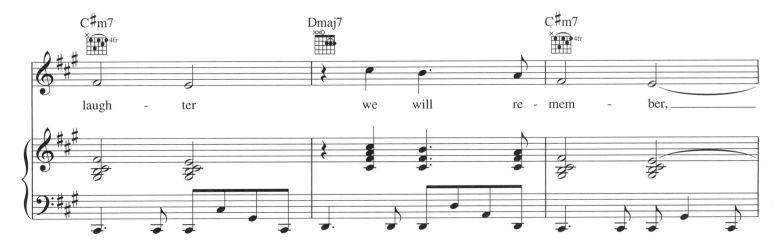

laugh - ter we will re - mem - ber,

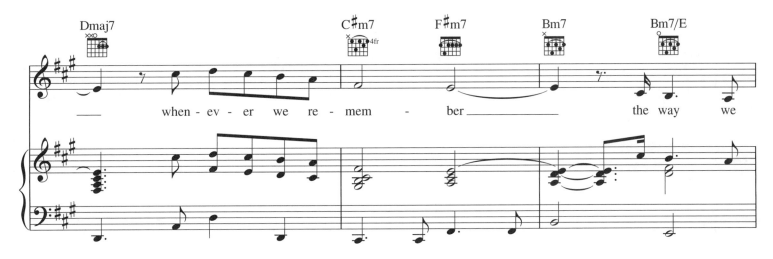

when - ev - er we re - mem - ber the way we

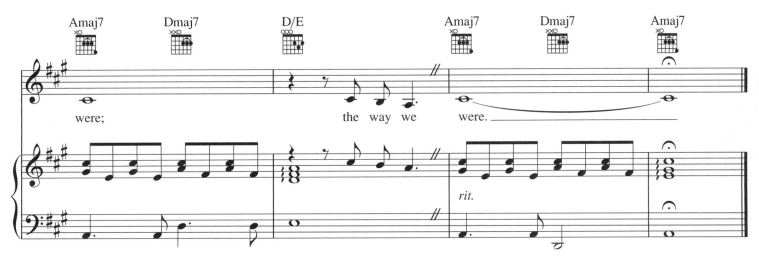

were; the way we were.

What a Wonderful World

featured in the Motion Picture GOOD MORNING VIETNAM

Words and Music by
George David Weiss and Bob Thiele

"What a won - der - ful world." _____ I see

skies of blue and clouds of white, the bright _____ bless-ed day, the

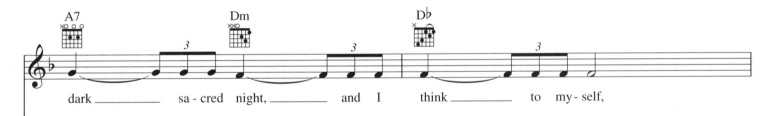

dark _____ sa - cred night, _____ and I think _____ to my- self,

"What a won - der - ful world." _____ The

col - ors of the rain - bow, so pret - ty in the sky, are

al - so on the fac - es of peo - ple go - in' by. I see

friends shak - in' hands, _____ say - in', "How do you do?"

They're real - ly say - in', "I love you." I hear

Where Do I Begin

(Love Theme)
from the Paramount Picture LOVE STORY

Words by Carl Sigman

Music by Francis Lai

Slowly

Where do I be-gin _____ to tell the sto-ry of how
With her first hel-lo _____ she gave a mean-ing to this

great a love can be, _____ the sweet love sto-ry that is
emp-ty world of mine. _____ There'd nev-er be an-oth-er

old-er than the sea, the sim-ple truth a-bout the
love, an-oth-er time; she came in-to my life and

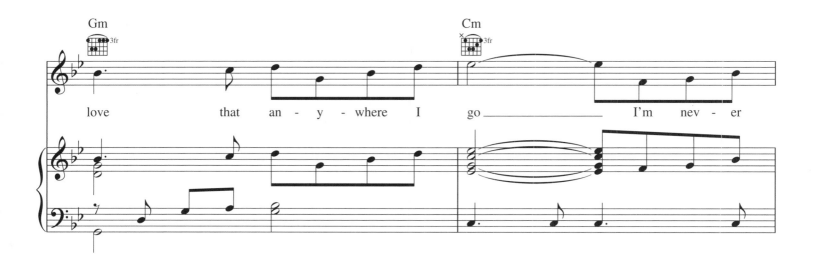

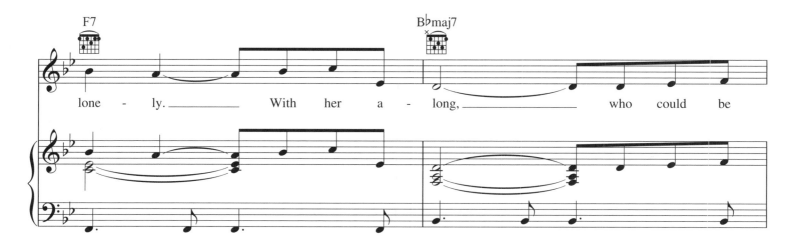

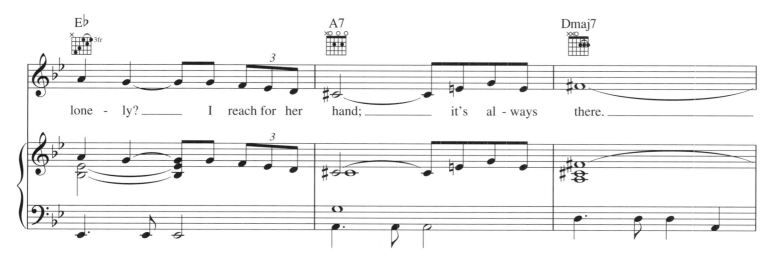

ho-urs in a day? _____ I have no an-swers now, but this much I can say:

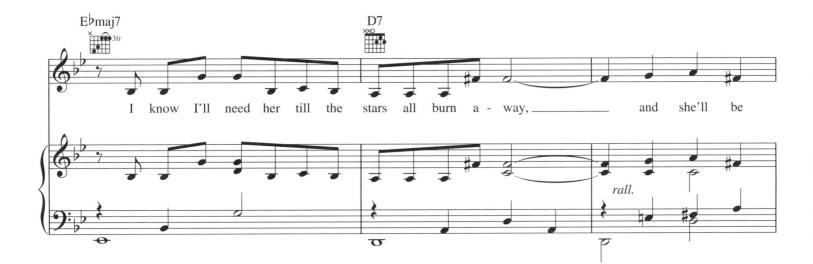

I know I'll need her till the stars all burn a-way, _____ and she'll be

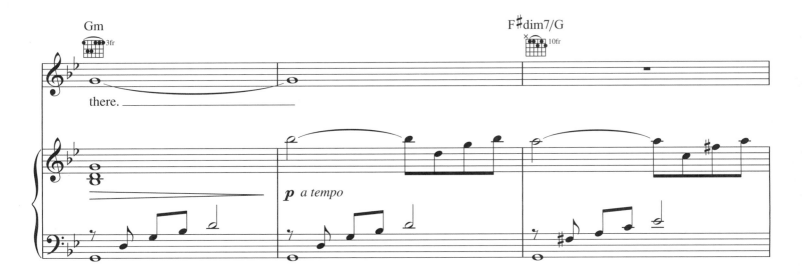

there. _____

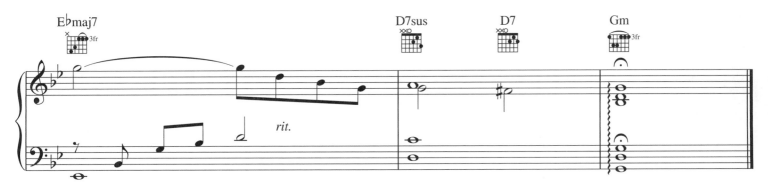

The Wind Beneath My Wings

from the Original Motion Picture BEACHES

Words and Music by
Larry Henley and Jeff Silbar

you al-ways walked___ the step be-hind.___

I was the one___ with all the glo - ry,

while you were the one___ with all the strength,

on-ly a face___ with-out a name,

Lyrics:

I nev-er once___ heard you com-plain.

Did you ev-er know___ that you're my___ he-ro,

and ev-'ry-thing___ I'd like to be?

I can fly high - er than an ea - gle,___

The Windmills of Your Mind

Theme from THE THOMAS CROWN AFFAIR

Words by
Alan and Marilyn Bergman

Music by Michel Legrand

Gmaj7   Cmaj7   F#m7♭5

moon.
stream. } Like a clock whose hands are sweep-ing past the min-utes of its face, And the world is like an

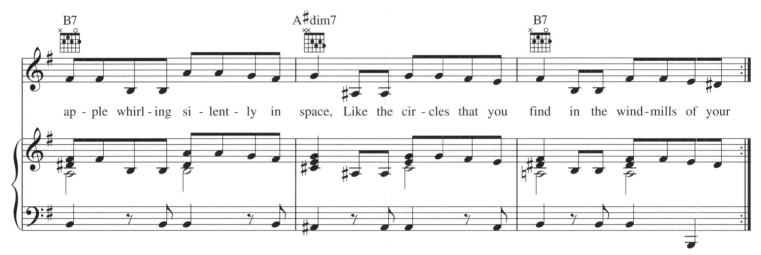

B7   A#dim7   B7

ap - ple whirl-ing si - lent-ly in space, Like the cir - cles that you find in the wind-mills of your

Em

mind! Keys that jin - gle in your pock - et, words that jan - gle in your

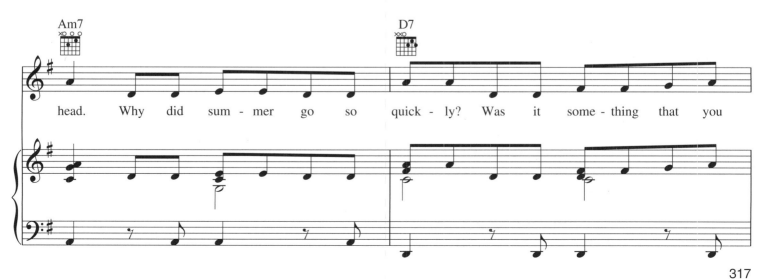

Am7   D7

head. Why did sum - mer go so quick - ly? Was it some - thing that you

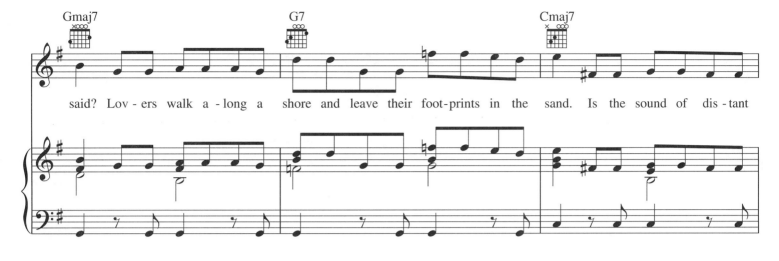

said? Lov-ers walk a-long a shore and leave their foot-prints in the sand. Is the sound of dis-tant

drum-ming just the fin-gers of your hand? Pic-tures hang-ing in a

hall-way and the frag-ment of a song. Half re-mem-bered names and fac-es, but to whom do they be-

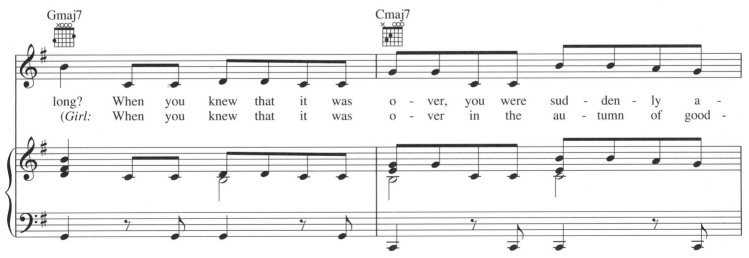

long? When you knew that it was o-ver, you were sud-den-ly a-
(*Girl:* When you knew that it was o-ver in the au-tumn of good-

THE **MOST** REQUESTED SERIES FROM

1112